WAYPOINT

WAYPOINT

NAVIGATING YOUR SPIRITUAL JOURNEY

Bob Whitesel

wesleyan
publishing
house

Indianapolis, Indiana

Copyright © 2010 by Bob Whitesel
Published by Wesleyan Publishing House
Indianapolis, Indiana 46250
Printed in the United States of America
ISBN: 978-0-89827-432-5

Library of Congress Cataloging-in-Publication Data

Whitesel, Bob.
Waypoint : navigating your spiritual journey / Bob Whitesel.
    p. cm. -- (Waypoint)
Includes bibliographical references.
ISBN 978-0-89827-432-5
1. Faith development. I. Title.
BT771.3.W45 2010
253.5'3--dc22
                                        2010019480

To travelers who seek solace and meaning.
To my family for helping me when the road became difficult.
To the One who illuminates my route.

Our battered suitcases were piled on the sidewalk again; we had longer ways to go. But no matter, the road is life.

—Jack Kerouac

CONTENTS

INTRODUCTION

Life seen as a journey, an ascent, a pilgrimage,
a road, is an idea as old as man himself.

—Esther de Waal[1]

Every traveler on life's journey will eventually ask the same basic questions: "Why am I here? What am I put here to do? Is there a purpose behind my existence?" As a fellow traveler, I believe there is something worth seeking behind all of these questions.

We may assume we are on a journey through life, but most of us don't seem particularly concerned about the direction, let alone the destination of that journey. We're that way for a while, anyway.

But eventually, often because of circumstances beyond our control, we realize that there has to be some direction, some purpose to it all. I believe this purpose can only come into focus if we study the map of our lives—where we have been and where we are going.

That is why this book looks closely at the road of life that all of us travel. It follows the wanderings and discoveries of one particular traveler: Oksana. Through her journey, we will discover several common features of that road of life. I've labeled those common features "Waypoints."

As one voyager said, "As a human race we are on a journey, and we need to know the road."[2]

OKSANA'S JOURNEY IS YOURS

Oksana's spiritual quest seems to begin quite by accident, in the outback of Australia. She could not predict the surprising journey she is about to travel. And yet, ironically, though lost in an inhospitable wilderness with scant hope for rescue, she will begin to find her spiritual way.

In the following chapters, we will follow Oksana's journey through life. It will not be easy or direct. Yet she will pass many waypoints— places along the road that all travelers must encounter. So in Oksana's journey, we may find clues to our own spiritual waypoints. And thus, Oksana's waypoints can become a roadmap for us.

WHAT ARE WAYPOINTS?

Satellites have created a Global Positioning System (GPS) that allows users of hand-held GPS units to track their position within thirty feet. When using a GPS unit, a traveler can mark a memorable location as a waypoint. The GPS unit will assign a precise longitude and latitude to this location. The traveler can then share this waypoint with other travelers so they can experience this exact location too.

So, when travelers encounter a special location on their journey, they can mark this location as a waypoint and share it with others. Waypointing is the marking and sharing of waypoints so that fellow travelers can share the joys, as well as note the similarities, of their own journeys.

WHAT ARE SPIRITUAL WAYPOINTS?

Many travelers have observed that life's journey seems to be guided by spiritual forces, hinting at an intersection of the supernatural and the natural. Almost every traveler has experienced what one traveler has described as "the sense or awareness—sometimes quiet, sometimes frenzied, but always a bit uncanny—of *Something* . . . as a feeling or even a sense—even a kind of sensation—of a presence that is . . . wholly other, absolute, overpowering, and divine."[3] In chapter 1, Oksana experiences this, and so begins her encounter with "the tremendous mystery" that would lead her down a path of many more waypoints.[4]

I have chosen to describe such common spiritual occurrences, which most travelers encounter, as spiritual waypoints. A spiritual waypoint tells where a traveler is in relation to the beginning and end of the spiritual quest. It gives an indication of a general position on life's journey.

SOME THINGS STAY THE SAME, REGARDLESS OF THE ROUTE

WAYPOINTS USUALLY UNFOLD IN THE SAME ORDER. Waypoints usually unfold in the order described in this book, counting down from Waypoint 16 to Waypoint 0.

WAYPOINTS CANNOT BE SKIPPED. Some of my friends feel they have skipped or circumvented certain waypoints. But upon closer inspection, it becomes clear that they did pass that way. Often a traveler does not notice a certain spiritual waypoint because it had happened quickly or in conjunction with another experience. To progress in the journey, one must travel through the next waypoint.

WAYPOINTS ALLOW COMPANIONS TO JOIN AND HELP YOU. Waypoints allow us to chart our journey and for companions to meet us en route.

WAYPOINTING IS CRITICAL FOR NOT GETTING LOST. Waypointing, the plotting out of waypoints, can help travelers see where they are in relation to the bigger picture of life's road. Waypointing helps travelers understand which waypoint they have passed and which will come next. Without charting the waypoints, travelers may: (a) get lost on life's journey, or (b) not see the progress they are making.

ALL TRAVELERS EXPERIENCE THE SAME BEGINNING AND END. Every traveler begins at Waypoint 16 without the knowledge of "a presence that is . . . wholly other, absolute, overpowering, and divine."[5] And in similar fashion, every traveler of life's journey will one day pass through this life and into death at Waypoint 0.

SOME THINGS VARY ON EACH ROUTE

WAYPOINTS APPEAR AT DIFFERENT LOCATIONS FOR EACH TRAVELER. Because the precise route of life's journey varies for each traveler, spiritual waypoints will appear in the same order, but can appear in a different locale for each person; that is, indigenously and personally.

WAYPOINTS ARE NOT SPACED EQUALLY APART. For some travelers, a waypoint may occur immediately after a previous waypoint. For others, an upcoming waypoint may take more time to reach.

WAYPOINTS ARE ENCOUNTERED AT DIFFERENT SPEEDS. For each traveler, this journey will unfold at a different pace. Some may take a lifetime to travel between Waypoint 16 and Waypoint 6. Others may travel between Waypoints 16 and 6 in their youth. There is no correct speed. All travel at the pace that is right for them. Travelers should not despair if their journey unfolds slowly, but rather each should celebrate the experiencing of life's journey.

The road of life is different for each traveler in length, route, and pace. Yet the same beginning, destination, and waypoints will always occur . . . for every one of us so long as we persevere in the journey.

So, let the waypointing begin.

—Bob Whitesel D.Min., Ph.D.
www.bobwhitesel.com

AWARENESS

We are all visitors to this time, this place. We are just passing
through. Our purpose here is to observe, to learn,
to grow, to love . . . and then we return home.

—Australian Aboriginal proverb

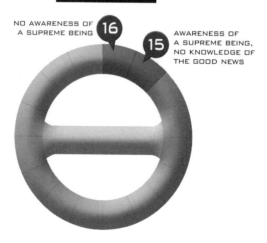

NO AWARENESS OF
A SUPREME BEING **16**

15 AWARENESS OF
A SUPREME BEING,
NO KNOWLEDGE OF
THE GOOD NEWS

THE NEVER-NEVER

The scraping grew louder as the wind pressed against the sides of the tent. It was common for morning winds to blow with such ferocity in these southern climates, but not before dawn. And it was still several hours until sunrise. The exhausted traveler buried her face once again in the folds of her sleeping bag. But now slumber eluded her because her thoughts returned to the images of the night before.

The ring of human bodies had appeared otherworldly. The lightning of an approaching storm seemed to suspend the dancers in a flash of white, and then return them to the fire's reddish glow. These were the First Nations people of Australia, a proud yet waning culture living in a region of the Australian outback that the locals call "the Never-Never." The ring dance had been the culmination of a night of storytelling and singing. And though Oksana had come to research their culture, what struck her most were their stories of Gulingi. "He is the creator," one told her. "He is sendin' us that storm. He's not there with the storm. We never see him. He's way, way back, sendin' it out to us. Sendin' his rain to us, sendin' the lightnin,' sendin' his life to us."[1]

Suddenly, Oksana awoke, not even realizing she had drifted back to sleep. Her Aboriginal hosts had departed. And so had the storm.

NOT ALONE

The day before, the wind had been her most frequent companion as she approached the waypoint where she would meet her hosts. And though the First Nations peoples and the storm had left sometime during the night, the wind had remained. *How interesting*, she thought. *These people worship a god they see in nature and feel through the wind, but who never communicates with them. They are on the verge of losing their way of life to the encroachment of civilization. How ironic that their god could not protect this incredible culture.*

She was not alone in her feelings about the god or its absence. A few months earlier she had mulled over an online article which declared that "the U.S. population continues to show signs of becoming less religious . . . The 'Nones' (no stated religious preference, atheist, or agnostic) continue to grow."[2] The "Nones" . . . that described her perfectly: no stated religious preference, open to everything, yet embracing nothing.

BEGINNINGS

Oksana's journey had begun two years earlier during a course at a local community college. Her instructor had been a man of magnificent travels who reveled in tales of voyages and treks into undiscovered corners of humanity. He was an anthropologist whose specialty was the stories of dying cultures and tribes. This passion led her to follow his footsteps to the Northern Territory of Australia. Here, she hoped to describe, and perhaps even write a book about, the amazing Aboriginal cultures. Yet as Oksana recorded their customs and dances that night, she began to sense an unseen theme. She noticed that in this inhospitable land where crops rarely thrive and food was even scarcer, these people embraced a hope that she somehow envied. Amid all of this uncertainty, they had a confidence—an assurance—that something was working on their behalf.

Oksana longed for such a feeling. She had embarked on this trip to become a writer. It was her route to financial security and emotional safety. Yet these First Nations people had none of the security she sought, but they still appeared content and confident.

WAYPOINT 16: WHAT IS IT?

What is a waypoint? It is a location that a traveler has marked with latitude and longitude coordinates so that others can find that exact location too. Waypoints may be a specific feature along the way such as a waterfall, mountain top, or canyon. And they can be a location where the traveler has an experience, such as a place where a dangerous animal or a hazard was encountered. Marking a waypoint and sharing it with others (sometimes called waypointing) is a way to ensure that others will either find the waypoint or avoid it.

Though Oksana did not call it waypointing, that's what she was doing as she recorded in her journal the experiences that began in the Never-Never and would culminate in an incredible journey that she never anticipated.

OKSANA'S ENCOUNTER AT WAYPOINT 16

Waypoint 16 is a time in a traveler's life where he or she has no awareness of a supreme being. Oksana had begun her journey here, a point where she had no knowledge of a god, nor had she sought one. She had developed a well-founded cynicism for the pious religion of her Midwestern upbringing. She had recently read a book titled *God Is Not Great: How Religion Poisons Everything*. She knew first-hand what the author talked about when he said that "the whole racket of American evangelism was just that: a heartless con run by the second-string characters from Chaucer's *Pardoner's Tale*. (You saps keep the faith. We'll just keep the money.)"[3]

This journey to Australia was her route to finding an alternative understanding of the world, one without a god and one without religion. It was during the evening with her Aboriginal hosts, however, that Oksana began to sense that something held these people together. She could only describe it as a wind that blew beneath and through all that these people did and hoped. The presence of that wind frightened and intrigued her. And for a moment, she wished to just leave this mysterious land and return to the comfort of familiar faces and places.

A day earlier in Tennant Creek, she began to record her travels in what she would later call her waypoint journal. On the first page, she wrote:

Before the Never-Never

God is a heartless con.

The Never-Never

I describe their hope as a wind that blows beneath and through all that these people do. The presence of that wind intrigues me.

From where does such confidence arise?

WAYPOINT 15: ABANDONED

Upon the heels of this tension between fascination and flight, leaving was suddenly no longer an option. That morning, she found her Jeep almost useless. Sometime during the previous day's drive, a leak had developed in the radiator. While she was reveling at the dance and merriment the night before, her Jeep was slowly losing its coolant. Her first clue was a sweet smell that lured her from the folds of her sleeping bag. She quickly discovered a dark green patch of sand underneath her Jeep, which indicated radiator fluid had seeped into the ground. She peered into the radiator. Though she could not see any fluid, she hoped that enough remained to aid her trip back to Tennant Creek.

Within minutes, she was bouncing down what could barely pass for a road. The day before, she had taken this road westward when the slanting rays of the sun illuminated a faint trail. But now as the sun rose, the trail was barely visible. Soon the bumps and jolts seemed more frequent than the day before, and she wondered if she had strayed off path. Soon her concern became pointless, for regardless of the route, the white steam that came from the engine told her another journey was about to begin.

LOST IN THE STARS

Night came quickly for Oksana. In her haste, she had left most of her supplies at the camp, hoping to reach Tennant Creek by nightfall. She had not planned to stay another night, and the evening before, she had gleefully shared most of her food with her Aboriginal hosts. Now, their revelry and songs seemed long gone, even foolish. Many miles from civilization and perhaps on the wrong trail, she was alone, hungry, and cold.

Though slumber eluded her for hours, she eventually fell asleep. But something woke her—a dim light emerging faintly from beyond a nearby hill. She wondered why such a faint light could rouse her from slumber. Digging behind the seat she found her small hiker's headlamp, and attaching its elastic band around her forehead, she stumbled out of the Jeep for a closer look.

A dim path seemed to be pressed into the low-lying grass, leading back and to the left from where she had come. It could not have been the Jeep's tracks, for it appeared much narrower and lighter. *Perhaps this is rescue*, she thought. *The dim glow might be an Aboriginal fire.* Though it was a dark and treacherous land, this seemed her best hope of rescue.

Following the path over a first low hill, the glow slowly disappeared, but the path grew clearer. She became convinced that this path was human-made, and must lead to somewhere more occupied that the ravine in which she had spent the first part of the night. Soon the path turned to the left again, this time more sharply, plunging between two rock faces into a narrow gorge. As the rock walls narrowed to within arm's distance, she sensed that they were covered with some kind of dark moss. Lifting her headlamp, she reeled in astonishment. These rock walls were covered with rock engravings that her professor called "petroglyphs." As she spun around almost in panic, she was surrounded by a painted whirlwind of warriors, hunters, families, and children. These were the stories of the Aboriginal people she had danced among the night before. This was their library, and these were their stories.

Once again, the self-reliance of these people impressed her. They were pictured as industrious, yet loving. And they seemed to have a sense of reliance that came from their understanding of nature, and maybe something behind it. She had listened to the elders the night before describe their "dreamtime," a period when their ancient ancestors created the world and named the animals. *How strange*, she thought. *This dreamtime sounds like the stories I remember from Sunday school: God creating a world, and his children giving names to the animals.* And then she looked upward to the stars, which now seemed to twinkle overhead with a nearness she could almost touch.

She sat down at the base of the great rocks and began writing in her journal again:

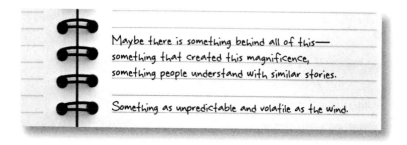

Maybe there is something behind all of this—something that created this magnificence, something people understand with similar stories.

Something as unpredictable and volatile as the wind.

Then reality returned. She was in a narrow canyon, many miles from the nearest town. She was alone, without transportation, and helpless. But strangely, she was at peace.

HOW TO NAVIGATE WAYPOINT 16

The waypoints Oksana is encountering are the same ones that all people will encounter. Waypoint 16 is a place where all travelers begin. It is a place where knowledge of God is not perceived or needed, and therefore, is not sought. But hints abound, and an

16

NO AWARENESS OF A SUPREME BEING
The traveler does not sense a supreme being is present or needed.

awareness begins to grow that there may be some greater purpose or power behind life's journey. These hints are similar to signposts that point toward the next waypoint.

16-A SOMETHING PERSONAL IN THE PURPOSE

As Oksana discovered, there seems to be something more private and more intangible behind life's journey. Every traveler comes to decide if a deity is behind life, based upon intuition, experience, and life's road. Maybe you are one such traveler, straining to see life's purpose and destination, and who, if anyone or thing, sustains it.

But regardless of what is behind the journey, there seems to be a sense that this world is not the result of an infinite series of accidents. Rather, there seems to be a private beckoning that compels humans to explore the powers behind life's route. And even though Oksana was disillusioned with religion, it was in the Never-Never that she began to sense her personal destiny and perhaps a purpose behind it.

16-B MOVING BEYOND YOUR BASIC NEEDS

Before a traveler is ready to move beyond Waypoint 16 and even consider the possibility of a divine presence, he or she must be able to focus on spiritual questions. Humans usually won't have interest in divine questions if their basic needs are going unmet.[4]

The quest for basic physical needs such as a reliable source for food, water, and a place to sleep can take precedence over a person's spiritual quest. So, too, can various forms of addiction. Much of the world struggles to meet these basic needs every day. And according to psychologists, people won't have interest in spiritual matters until they are no longer preoccupied with meeting their basic needs.[5]

Those of us who have these basic needs met should be looking for opportunities to help others meet them. One great teacher said, "For everyone to whom much is given, from him much will be required."[6]

HOW TO NAVIGATE WAYPOINT 15

At this point, travelers may leave Waypoint 16 behind, a point where they are sure there is no god, and enter Waypoint 15 where they begin to be aware of a supreme being. Most travelers, like Oksana, begin to sense that God may exist. Here are a few common signposts that alert a traveler that he or she is nearing Waypoint 15.

> ### 15
> **AWARENESS OF A SUPREME BEING, NO KNOWLEDGE OF THE GOOD NEWS**
> The traveler begins to sense there is a god, but does not know who God is.

15-A A STORY EMERGES BEHIND ALL STORIES

In the encounter with the rituals and rock engravings of her Aboriginal hosts, Oksana observed stories that were similar to those she heard as a child in church. The Aborigines' creator whose children populated the earth[7] reminded her of the fatherly God walking in the garden of Eden with Adam and Eve. Just as Adam and Eve named the animals, so, too, the Aboriginal ancestors were given responsibility to name the animals in the dreamtime. Though imprecise, Oksana still felt there might be a common story behind the two versions.[8]

Another traveler named Jack Lewis described how he was surprised by joy at Waypoint 15.[9] A professor of medieval legends, Jack studied mythology and mysticism. And he began to notice similarities between many religious stories. Just as Oksana witnessed similarities between the religious stories of her Aboriginal hosts and her Sunday school lessons, Jack saw similarities between hundreds of religious myths. Jack eventually concluded that there must be one basic and true story that was behind these many variations.[10]

This led Jack to believe that there was a story behind all stories, though he was still not sure which story was the original. Was it Buddhism, Taoism, Islam, Judaism, Christianity, or some other less-worn path? That decision would have to wait for Jack and you because there are more waypoints ahead before the purpose behind the journey will come into view.

But Jack summed up his feelings at Waypoint 15 this way: "A drop of disturbing doubt fell into my Materialism. It was merely a 'Perhaps.' Perhaps (oh joy!) there was, after all, 'something else.'"[11]

15-B A GLIMMER OF GOOD IS SEEN IN OTHERS

Sometimes a traveler will detect a glimmer of good in others that leads him or her to sense that there must be a good god behind the good actions. A great teacher once suggested that good actions would allow others to see this divine spark: "I was hungry and you fed me, I was thirsty and you gave me a drink, I was homeless and you gave me a room, I was shivering and you gave me clothes, I was sick and you stopped to visit, I was in prison and you came to me." His followers had never seen him in such need. And they replied, "Master, what are you talking about? When did we ever see you hungry and feed you, thirsty and give you a drink? And when did we ever see you sick or in prison and come to you?" The great teacher replied, "I'm telling the solemn truth: Whenever you did one of these things to someone overlooked or ignored, that was me—you did it to me.[12]

One day, hospitals would be founded in this teacher's name, prisons accessed, and charitable deeds undertaken, neither lauded nor remembered. Such benevolent action on behalf of others can hint at a divine motivation. Good deeds, such as standing in solidarity with the needy, can hint that there is some supernatural power behind such selfless persistence and commitment. The good that others exhibit does not necessarily come from a divine spark, but it can be an indication that passion for others has been divinely lit.

15-C THE MAGNIFICENCE OF GOD-CRAFT

Many travelers have exclaimed, "There has to be a god, because, well, the universe couldn't just happen." As Oksana discovered, there is a sense that some force is behind the design and cause of the universe.[13] For ages, humankind has looked at the universe and sensed that something created its splendor. Three thousand years ago, a poet wrote: "God's glory is on tour in the skies, God-craft on exhibit across the horizon."[14]

Is there a god behind the beginning of the universe?

When considering the universe's beginning, most travelers will recall the big bang theory, where the universe is created in an instant flash of light and energy.[15] But belief in the big bang does not preclude that a god could be behind it. The famous astronomer Robert Jastrow wrote, "The details differ, but the essential elements in the astronomical (Big Bang theory) and biblical accounts of Genesis are the same: the chain of events leading to man commenced suddenly and sharply at a definite movement in time, in a flash of light and energy."[16]

Even avowed atheist and philosopher Kai Nielsen admits he is mystified by how a big bang could rise from nothing. Nielsen states, "Suppose you suddenly hear a loud bang . . . and you ask me, 'What made that bang?' and I reply, 'Nothing, it just happened.' You would not accept that. In fact you would find my reply quite unintelligible."[17] Another scientist who is often critical of religion, Stephen Hawking, concludes, "The odds against a universe like ours emerging out of something like the Big Bang are enormous. I think there are clearly religious implications when you start to discuss the origins of the universe. There must be religious overtones."[18]

Is there a god behind the fine-tuning of the universe?

Seven hundred years ago a writer summed up that "some intelligent being exists, by whom all natural things are directed."[19] By this he meant that an intelligent force must be guiding the universe because the universe works together so harmoniously and with such precision.

Francis Collins, a geneticist tapped by President Obama to be Director of the National Institutes of Health, points out that there are fifteen constants or universal laws of nature that "if any one of the constants were off by even one part in a million . . . there would have been no galaxy, stars, planets or people."[20] Collins concluded, "When you look at that evidence, it is very difficult to adopt the view that [the universe] was just chance."[21]

15-D WHERE WE HAVE BEEN AND WHAT LIES AHEAD

Waypoint 16 is experienced when a belief in a god is not needed nor perceived. But Waypoint 15 is reached when story, good deeds, creation, or an assortment of other signposts lead the traveler into entertaining the possibility that there may be a god.

Experience seems to point to even more waypoints up ahead, where something more grand, more personal, and more exciting awaits. The usual explanation is that this is a god and some sort of purpose is involved. If the traveler reading this book is entertaining that conclusion, then press on to chapter 2.

But if the traveler is not convinced that a deity of some sort exists, then the traveler may need to wait at this juncture and watch.

QUESTIONS FOR PERSONAL REFLECTION

Begin waypointing by drawing a map of your spiritual journey (like the figure on page 15) in your own personal waypoint journal. Your drawing could look like a timeline across a sheet of paper. The left end of the timeline should depict the beginning of your spiritual journey. And the right end should depict its end. Use your journal and chart to respond to questions for personal reflection throughout this book.

1. How did you experience Waypoint 16 and 15 in your own life? Write a short description and locate each on your waypoint map.
2. Do you recall a time when you experienced nature in its splendor? How did it make you feel? Did you feel more alone or less alone?
3. Do you sense that there is some deity behind the design or meaning of this life? If so, then you have passed beyond Waypoint 15. Journey on to the next two chapters and discover what waypoints are ahead.

FLASH

A journey is best measured in friends, rather than miles.
—Tim Cahill[1]

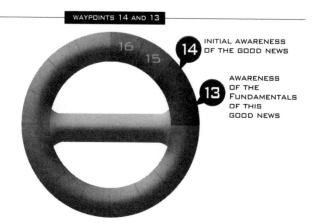

14 INITIAL AWARENESS OF THE GOOD NEWS

13 AWARENESS OF THE FUNDAMENTALS OF THIS GOOD NEWS

AWAKE

The sound of burbling water lulled Oksana from her sleep. Aside from a splitting headache, she seemed fine . . . but drenched in water. Stroking her hair back from her eyes, she realized this was not water, but blood. "Where is Jacob?" she tried to shout, but only a soft murmur came from her throat. Try as she may, she was unable to speak. And then, as quickly as she awoke, she drifted back into a fitful sleep.

Years before, Oksana was wandering lost among the Aboriginal rock paintings when she was discovered by a local outfitter named Jon. After a whirlwind courtship in Melbourne, they were married. However, before Oksana even learned that Jacob was on the way, their marriage began dissolving and eventually ended in divorce. Soon after, she returned to Chicago and to the local community college where she would eventually meet Arjan.

When Oksana awoke again, she was lying in an unfamiliar room. She seemed to recall that her high school prom was the night before. Rolling over to look around, she was startled by a strange man with a full, dark beard, olive skin, and a mass of black curly hair sleeping next to her. Oksana's eyes began to tear. *How can this be?* she wondered. *I've never slept with a man. How could this happen on the night of my prom?*

The man stirred. As Oksana quietly struggled to pull herself to the edge of the bed, a large muscular hand grasped hers and pulled her back. In a voice both deep and familiar, he whispered, "There, there. You'll feel better in a minute." Thrashing and prying herself away from this man and his bed, Oksana fell to the floor with a thud.

Suddenly, footsteps could be heard on the stairs outside the room, and bursting through the door was an old woman. The woman bore a strange resemblance to Oksana's grandmother, but was different still. "Were you hurt?" the woman cried, and dropped to Oksana's side. As Oksana crumpled into the woman's arms, a strangely warm voice assured her, "We are here now. Don't worry; your husband and I are here for you. Come, we better return to the hospital." The word *husband* stunned Oksana even more than the thought of being violated. "Where am I? And where is Jacob?"

On the way to the hospital, the man sat uncomfortably close. "There was a break-in at our house," he began softly. "You were unconscious by the pool with a gaping wound on your head and bruises to your neck. You said you confronted two intruders. They attacked you and you hit your head. But when they heard Jacob crying, they ran."

This was news to Oksana. The last thing she remembered was going to bed the night before, after her high school prom. *Who is this man? Am I married? Is this some cover up for rape? Why take me to the hospital? And why isn't Jacob here?*

Once at the hospital, Oksana began to grasp a story as fantastic as it was implausible. Oksana was not seventeen years old as she believed, but over a decade older. At twenty-eight, she had been married for four years, and the strange man was her husband, Arjan. And though she could recall everything before her prom, she had no memory of the eleven years since. Soon a nurse entered and introduced herself as Jaci Gaspar. "The doctor ordered a sedative, and it's time for you to sleep." Inwardly, such a prospect terrified Oksana. "What if I lose more of my memory when I sleep?"

THREE GUIDES

When Oksana awoke, Arjan and another man were seated near her bed. As she stirred, Arjan grasped her hand. Though Oksana's memories of her previous encounter with Arjan were recalled, she had no further memories of Arjan or anything that happened in the missing eleven years. "Why is he here?" were the first words Oksana could remember clearly saying, pointing to the unknown man still slumbering in the nearby chair. "Udham is a spiritual teacher, a minister of Sikh Dharma," said Arjan. "Six months ago, you began the process of converting to

Sikhism, and he is our teacher." Oksana could recall the revivalism in the small churches of her youth, but she had never heard nor encountered anyone who was a Sikh. "Why would I be doing this?" she replied almost beneath her breath.

Over the next few days, Oksana came to understand and even appreciate the quiet and patient love of Arjan. Arjan had brought to her the waypoint journal, and in it she discovered loving passages describing Arjan. Yet none of these stories rekindled her love. She wrote in her journal:

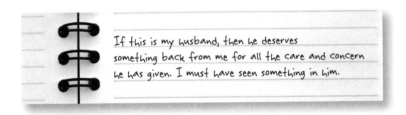

If this is my husband, then he deserves
something back from me for all the care and concern
he has given. I must have seen something in him.

Though unfamiliar, she obliged Udham's stories of his Sikh culture. The ten gurus and their stories captivated her. She came to see a story of respect and love emerging from Udham's daily discourses. "But aren't there other ways to God?" she blurted out one day. Though Oksana had rejected the religion of her youth, she was not yet ready to accept this unfamiliar yet fascinating way. "Arjan, I want to learn more. More about all religions. More about all gods. Please Arjan, please." With so much of her past still missing, Oksana had become reluctant to make life-altering decisions.

Yet Arjan's kindness toward Oksana was boundless. He brought a stack of books about most of the major religions from the library. In what would become an extended hospital stay, Oksana began to refill those empty recesses of her mind, and she began to fill them with stories of religion.

During this time, three visitors became regulars to Oksana's room. Udham continued his daily visits, sharing stories of Sikhism. It became clear to Oksana that Arjan wanted her desperately to join him in his faith. And this made these daily encounters all the more attractive, for Arjan was becoming a friend and confidant. She even thought that she might be starting to love Arjan, and she was growing in admiration for his religion as well.

Another regular visitor was her nurse, Jaci. A nun of the Sisters of the Holy Cross, she had dedicated her life to helping others at St. John's Hospital. Jaci had a deep, yet quiet faith. Still, Oksana drew it out by daily pestering Jaci with questions. In return, Jaci opened up for Oksana a whole new understanding of Christianity. Jaci emphasized to Oksana that her quest for God was an important search. Paraphrasing one of her favorite writers, Jaci said, "If religion is false, then your quest to find it is of no importance. But, if religion is true, then your search is very important. The one thing your search for God cannot be is moderately important."

Jaci also possessed what Oksana described in her journal as "a gift of poetry and storytelling." Jaci recounted the biblical stories as if they happened yesterday. And Jaci painted a picture of a future heaven without fear, anxiety, or death. "What a perfect place," Oksana concluded. But Jaci responded, "God put us here to help others. You cannot shorten your time on this earth, no matter how difficult it may be. We must make the most of the time we're given and serve others." This service to others impressed Oksana the most. She watched as Jaci and the Sisters spent long hours in care of the infirm and dying. The dogged persistence of these Sisters of the Holy Cross was almost otherworldly. And in these actions, Oksana began to see a glimmer of good in the faith she had rejected as a child.

Abdel-Halim was the third regular visitor. Oksana had been impressed with his passion for God. Frankly, his stories were the most enthusiastic, heroic, and valiant she had heard. He described Mohammed's encounter with the archangel in a cave near Mecca and Mohammed's hatred of the idolatry and immorality of his Arab neighbors. "Islam is the youngest of the major religions, but one of the largest," concluded Abdel-Halim at the end of one discussion, adding "one and a half billion followers means something." The number of travelers on this path impressed Oksana almost more than any of the previous stories.

CHOICES

Amid these choices, Oksana was soon confronted with another. "You can go now," said her doctor. *But where?* she wondered. Oksana was not ready to rejoin Arjan in his home, much less share his bed. But he was the closest thing she had to a friend. And he had stood by her. "Where else would I go?" she responded to the doctor, half hoping he might offer some alternative. When none was given, she responded "That's fine." And her depression grew again.

On the way home in the car, Oksana thought about how her life must have been. Through her conversations with Arjan, she learned how they had met after her return home to Chicago from Australia, and that he had been a student at her community college. She discovered he was almost fifteen years her senior, but also that he was a good and caring man. But what choices had brought her to this place in life, she still could not fathom. She learned that she was married once before to Jon, whom she also didn't remember, and Jacob was their child.

It was with some despondency that she walked up the sidewalk to Arjan's house. Upon reaching the doorstep, the door burst open and there was the aging woman she had come to know as her mother. Holding a struggling eighteen-month-old squirming child, she put him down and he stumbled toward Oksana. Something in Oksana drew her irresistibly to this child. And she impulsively snatched him into her arms. "Jacob," she said quietly, surprising even herself. "Now dear," came her mother's reply. "Make the most of the time. He has to return to Jon at five o'clock."

How to Navigate Waypoint 14

At this point in Oksana's spiritual journey, she has encountered Waypoint 14, a place where a person first gains an awareness of various religions. Oksana's looming conversion to Sikhism compelled her to study

> **14**
>
> INITIAL AWARENESS OF THE GOOD NEWS
>
> The traveler becomes aware of good news about God through the deeds and words of his followers.

many religions. And in her conversations with Udham, Jaci, and Abdel-Halim, she encountered Waypoint 14.

Some people would like to ignore the question of God as long as possible. But Oksana had no such luxury. She awoke to find herself on the verge of religious conversion. To navigate Waypoint 14 it becomes important to wrestle with the important questions of religion and eternity.

14-A ▷ Wrestle with the Seriousness of Religion

Jack Lewis, whom Jaci paraphrased, understood the seriousness of religion when he argued, "Christianity is a statement which, if false, is of *no* importance, and, if true, of infinite importance. The one thing it cannot be is moderately important."[2] Using Christianity as an example, Jack was saying that if the biblical claims of eternal life[3] are true and that Jesus is the only way to eternal life,[4] then Christianity holds an all-important key to infinity that cannot be ignored.

14-B ▷ Wrestle with the Seriousness of Eternity

To grasp the seriousness of the future and to prepare for it, most people need a mental picture. The Bible is filled with passages that visualize a life after death.

- Jesus stated, "Do not let your hearts be troubled. Trust in God; trust also in me. In my Father's house are many rooms; if it were not so, I would have told you. I am going there to prepare a place for you. And if I go and prepare a place for you, I will come back and take you to be with me that you also may be where I am."[5]

- Peter, another follower of Jesus, said that supernatural happiness will outshine earthly wealth, stating that there is "an inheritance that can never perish, spoil or fade—kept in heaven for you."[6]

- Many books give amazing images of heaven and can be found in almost any public library. C. S. (Jack) Lewis's books *The Chronicles of Narnia* (especially the last book), *The Great Divorce* (especially the sections on heaven), and *The Space Trilogy* (especially the last book) are a few of his books that paint inspiring pictures of eternity. Even modern stories such as Trudy Harris's *Glimpses of Heaven: True Stories of Hope and Peace at the End of Life's Journey*, and Piper and Murphy's *90 Minutes in Heaven: A True Story of Death & Life* can help travelers at Waypoint 14 focus on the road ahead.

HOW TO NAVIGATE WAYPOINT 13

13

AWARENESS OF THE
BASICS OF THIS
GOOD NEWS
The traveler begins to
understand the basic
principles of various
religions.

Waypoint 13 occurs when a person becomes aware of the basic principles of various religions. It is here where travelers start seeing variations and disagreements between religions. Therefore, it is at Waypoint 13 that travelers begin to choose their different routes.[7]

At Waypoint 13, most travelers begin to list and compare the differences between religious viewpoints. Once spiritual curiosity has been stirred, they often launch into multiple religious directions. This if fine, for in investigating various religions, the true way can emerge.[8]

13-A TALK WITH RELIGIOUS PEOPLE

Oksana discovered that through dialogue with religious people, she could learn about the values, purposes, and benefits of each religion. Still, there are two warnings that should be considered.

DO NOT DIALOGUE WITH MANIPULATIVE AND SCHEMING PEOPLE. These are not authentic religious people, but rather people who have distorted religion to support their own need for recognition and power. You can recognize this in some of the following actions:

1. Too much power held by too few people.
2. Illogical and/or cruel laws or regulations.
3. Isolation from other people.[9]

TALK WITH AUTHENTIC AND HONEST RELIGIOUS PEOPLE. Most people can readily tell when a person is honest and genuine. Oksana felt such authenticity in her conversations with Udham, Jaci, and Abdel-Halim. It is important to dialogue with those people who will not act deceptively or turn the conversation into a tirade or rant. Rather, look for people who can explain their religion clearly, but also do so with civility.

13-B RELIGIOUS TERMINOLOGY MAY NEED TRANSLATION

When talking with religious people, a traveler may be bombarded with a specialized language. The traveler who is in conversation with religious people will need to undertake the following actions of translation.

ASK FOR CLARIFICATION. When you hear a word you do not understand, do not sit idly by, but say, "I don't understand. Can you explain it in different words?"

RESTATE TERMS IN YOUR OWN WORDS. Repeat to the religious person the unclear term or topic in your own words and ask, "Did I get that right?" Continue to restate the word until you and the religious person come to an agreement on the meaning.[10]

WRITE IT DOWN. Write down the word, your translation, and the date in your waypoint journal. Keep it for future reference.

13-C COMPARE RELIGIONS

During the weeks in the hospital and over the months at home, Oksana's memory did not return. And though the doctors thought more memories would surface before Christmas, Easter passed and still there were none. Jacob brightened her day with his playful inquisitiveness as she became acquainted with a child she could not remember carrying or birthing. Still, to pass the time and retain her sanity, Oksana continued her investigation into religion. The visits with Udham, Jaci, and Abdel-Halim became less frequent, but her interest grew keener. Devouring books on the subject of religions, Oksana scrawled a crude chart of comparisons in her waypoint journal. These would help her remember and compare what she had learned.

It should be noted that this figure is neither definitive nor exhaustive. These are simply Oksana's notes about the fundamentals of the faiths she encountered on her journey. You should create your own chart, but the following chart may be a fitting starting place.[11]

	Sikhism	Judaism	Christianity	Islam
God is...	One God, revealed through ten gurus. God is an impersonal power.	One God,[12] very fatherly yet stern.	One God with three personalities: fatherly (Father), loving (Son), and empowering (Holy Spirit).[13]	One God, stern and strict. Islam means "to accept, surrender or submit."
Who is Jesus?	Jesus is not God, but one who showed the "way" to God as did the ten gurus.	A good teacher, maybe a prophet; but not God's promised Messiah (Anointed One).	The promised Messiah (Anointed One and God's Son).[14] He died for our sins and rose to show power over death.[15]	A prophet, lesser than Mohammed.[16]

	Sikhism	Judaism	Christianity	Islam
How is Jesus viewed?	Jesus is just one of many ways to salvation.	Another good teacher, but not the Messiah.	God's messenger (Son and Messiah), and the only way to God.[17]	A prophet, but to say that Jesus is God is shirk or blasphemy.
Heaven?	A place of punishment or reward, but this is not the focus. Meditating upon God's name is the focus.	The heart of the earth (Sheol), a place of torment or comfort.[18]	A definite supernatural destiny. A place of community, goodness, happiness, and joy.	A place of community, goodness, and even sensual pleasures.
To reach heaven...	Meditate on the holy name, work diligently and share.	Follow God's laws and the teachings of great rabbis.	Follow Jesus' example and do good works, serve others, and follow God's laws.	Follow God's laws carefully and strictly.
How you connect to God.	Meditate and welcome others.	Adherence to ritual and tradition.	Serve others and grow in faith in Jesus.	Obedience to laws.
Countries where each religion is the dominant religion.	High population density with growing economic power. Converts not sought, but welcomed.	Separatist, and conversion not encouraged. Due to wrongs of the past, somewhat a fortress mentality.	Other religions are allowed, but Christianity tries to convert them by their intellect.	Other religions are discouraged, and Islam tries to convert them by physical force.
The bottom line.	One God known through meditating upon his name.	One God known through ritual and obedience.	One God (with three personalities) known through faith in God and service to others.	One God known through obedience and history.

QUESTIONS FOR PERSONAL REFLECTION

1. How did you experience Waypoint 14 and 13 (if you did)? In your waypoint journal, write a short description and locate each on your waypoint map.

2. If you are at Waypoint 14 or 13, who could you begin a discussion with about religion? What would you like to learn? What are you afraid you might learn? Set out to connect with such people and begin your own comparison of religions chart in your waypoint journal.

RELEVANCE

Existence is no more than the precarious attainment of relevance in
an intensely mobile flux of past, present, and future.

—Susan Sontag[1]

WAYPOINTS 12 AND 11

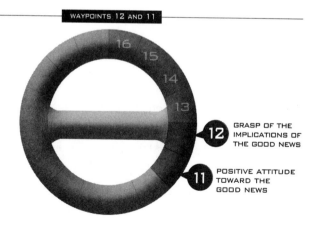

12 GRASP OF THE
IMPLICATIONS OF
THE GOOD NEWS

11 POSITIVE ATTITUDE
TOWARD THE
GOOD NEWS

FLUX

Six Christmases had come and gone, and still those eleven elusive years did not return. So, in their place, Oksana created new memories. And visiting Chicago's Miracle Mile with Jacob at Christmas was one of the fondest of her new memories. This Christmas the weather did not cooperate, spitting a wintery mix of rain and sleet. An icy sheen on the sidewalk made walking difficult, and to this was added the constant pulling of seven-and-a-half-year-old Jacob.

It was amid one of these tugs that Oksana lost her footing and tumbled to the ground. As quickly as she fell, Jacob darted and disappeared into the tangle of pedestrians along the sidewalk. As Oksana struggled to her feet, she caught sight of a large CTA bus swerving close to the pedestrians ahead. A gasp rang out from the crowd and Oksana shouted an agonizing prayer: "God help!"

Pushing aside the onlookers, she found Jacob safe but frightened by a near miss. Clutched in the arms of a Latina woman, he had begun to cry. Upon seeing Jacob safe, Oksana began to sob as they embraced. "Why did you keep pulling?" she scolded him. "Why? Why! You knew something like this could happen!" And without hesitation, almost in one breath with her prayer, Oksana slapped Jacob hard across the mouth. The gasp of the onlookers was either unnoticed or unheard by Oksana. All she could think was, *Why . . . why did I do that?*

The Latina woman remained with Oksana and Jacob as both sat on a nearby bench and cried. "My name is Francine," the woman softly offered. "I work nearby, and there is coffee and towels to dry yourself. Please, come and warm yourselves."

Soon Oksana found herself entering a metal door on a side street. For a moment, she hesitated, but a dim light at the end of the hall and the lyrical sounds of voices beckoned her. The hallway opened upon a small room where several Latina ladies were in animated conversation. Their conversation ended abruptly when Oksana and Jacob entered, but seeing the reddened eyes of Jacob and Oksana, the women immediately surrounded them with loving arms and unknown yet melodic tongues.

These were Francine's fellow employees, evening custodians at a large, Michigan Avenue department store. Though Oksana did not know Spanish, she grasped that the others would work for Francine that night, so that Francine could stay with Oksana and Jacob. Jacob had already fallen asleep in a worn, overstuffed chair in the far corner. Somehow, it seemed to Oksana that though Jacob felt at peace, he still wanted to remain some distance from Oksana.

"Why did I do that?" Oksana finally murmured to herself. Several minutes went by before Francine quietly replied, "I don't know, but I've done it too."

WEAKNESS

As Jacob slept, Oksana and Francine began what would become a long and extended conversation. It was nearly midnight before Francine put Oksana and Jacob in a cab to send them home. But before she departed, Oksana put a small note with her address in Francine's hand and said, "Please, let's talk more."

And their conversation continued over the next several months, sometimes at a café near where Francine lived, and sometimes at Oksana's home on the North Side.

It was these conversations with Francine that finally began to adequately fill the void of those eleven missing years. Oksana learned that Francine had been physically abused as a child, and that this had damaged her relationship with the cruel uncle who had raised her. And Oksana learned to her surprise that Francine too had become violent, as it was the only way she had learned to cope with anger, disappointment, and despair. Francine's worst memories were when, as a teenager, she had unleashed her anger and fists upon her younger brothers, creating a rift that eventually drove her from her home in Venezuela. Violence had ruined Francine's life, and she was determined not to let it ruin another.

These conversations gave Oksana a spark of hope. She was not alone in her battle. Francine credited her strength to a deep and abiding faith in God. She often peppered her conversations with Bible passages, which she looked up in her Spanish Bible and then translated as best she could. Oksana found Francine's translations reminiscent of Jaci's stories. But Francine, in sometimes broken English, often brought out the modern lessons better. Oksana came to value Francine's inelegant translations. She found them engaging, helpful, and surprisingly relevant.

One day as Francine was leaving Oksana's home, Tobias, a coworker of Arjan, stopped by. Upon the heels of another conversation with Francine, Oksana gushed to Tobias about her growing appreciation for the Bible. "You're kidding yourself Oksana," came Tobias's reply. "Christianity is a hoax for simple minds. It won't help. You need professional help—especially if you are going to get Arjan back."

How to Navigate Waypoint 12

12

GRASP OF THE IMPLICATIONS OF THE GOOD NEWS
Travelers begin to understand the good news has personal implications for them, and will require changes (for the good) in their life.

Waypoint 12 is reached when travelers begin to see that religion has implications for them personally. Oksana began to see in Francine's faith a power that she hoped would help her overcome her failings as a mother and spouse.

⟨12-A⟩ Life in a Post-Christian World

Oksana hoped she would receive Tobias's support when she gushed about her friend Francine and her faith. Yet Oksana received no such encouragement. Oksana was discovering that Christianity, once the dominant belief in North America, is today often ridiculed more than praised.[2] For good reason, some have described the present era as post-Christian.[3]

12-8 THE RELEVANCE OF THE BIBLICAL WORLDVIEW

Still Francine began a friendship and a discussion with Oksana. Both women had similar backgrounds, and this gave Francine's insights an authenticity with Oksana. It was with a friend, and at an unhurried pace, that Oksana began to grasp the implications of the Bible for her.

But Francine often used a word that confused and irritated Oksana. Francine would talk about the Bible being God's good news. But then at other times Francine would translate good news with the word *evangelism*. This last term annoyed Oksana, for it reminded her of her youth when evangelists would visit her small, Midwestern church. Though a few seemed authentic, it was the charlatans and self-centered preachers she remembered the most vividly. An evangelist was not someone with good news to Oksana.

A few weeks after Oksana's conversation with Tobias, Francine returned with another definition of good news.

"It means 'breaking news,' or a 'news flash,'" began Francine. "My priest said it was God's news that we could make a break with our past." This intrigued Oksana, for Francine's discussions were very good news. And over the months since that first meeting on Michigan Avenue, Francine shared the basics of her faith with no topics off-limits.

THE GOOD NEWS

Travelers who find themselves wanting to understand the basics of the Bible's good news can find them in several ways: by beginning a dialogue with a person who has been helped by the Bible's good news, by fellow-shipping with a community of faith that grasps the Bible's good news, or by looking up the basics in the following passages and books.

1. There is one God and creator who exists in space and time.
   * The Good News:
     o "And there is no God apart from me, a righteous God and a Savior; there is none but me. Turn to me and be saved, all you ends of the earth; for I am God, and there is no other."[4]
     o See also: Genesis 1–2; Exodus 15:11; 20:2–6; Deuteronomy 6:4; Isaiah 45:5–6; and Malachi 3:6.
   * Books:
     o *The Case for Christ* by Lee Strobel
     o "Why I Believe the God of the Bible is the One True God" in *Why I Am a Christian, Faith on Trial* edited by Paul Hoffman and Norman Geisler
2. Humans, because of willful acts of wrongdoing, destroy their relationship with the God who made them.
   * The Good News:
     o "For all have sinned and fall short of the glory of God."[5]
     o "If we claim to be without sin, we deceive ourselves."[6]
     o See also: Genesis 2:16–17; 3:7–8; Romans 3:9–18, 23; 6:23; and Ephesians 2:13–16.
   * Books:
     o *Tears of God* by Fr. Benedict Groeschel
     o *Know Why You Believe* by Paul E. Little
     o *Epic: The Story God is Telling* by John Eldridge
3. Jesus Christ is God's Son, who through his death and resurrection can forgive our sins and restore us to fellowship with God.
   * The Good News:
     o "If we claim to be without sin, we deceive ourselves and the truth is not in us. If we confess our sins, he is faithful and just and will forgive us our sins and purify us from all unrighteousness."[7]
     o See also: Isaiah 53:5; Matthew 1:21; John 1:29; 6:47; 14:6; Romans 5:8; 6:23; 2 Corinthians 5:21; Ephesians 2:8–9; Colossians 1:4; 1 Timothy 2:5; Hebrews 9:22; and 11:6.
   * Books:
     o "Why I Believe Jesus Is The Promised Messiah" and "Why I Believe Jesus Is the Son of God" in *Why I Am a Christian* edited by Paul Hoffman and Norman Geisler

- ○ *The Case for Christ* by Lee Strobel
- ○ *How to Give Away Your Faith* by Paul E. Little
- ○ *The Jesus I Never Knew* by Philip Yancy
4. The Bible is a valid witness to eternal spiritual truth.
- • The Good News:
  - ○ "There's nothing like the written Word of God for showing you the way to salvation through faith in Christ Jesus. Every part of Scripture is God-breathed and useful one way or another—showing us truth, exposing our rebellion, correcting our mistakes, training us to live God's way."[8]
  - ○ See also: Psalm 119 and Jude 3.
- • Books:
  - ○ "Why I Believe the Bible Alone Is the Word of God" in *Why I Am a Christian* edited by Paul Hoffman and Norman Geisler
  - ○ *The New Testament Documents: Are They Reliable?* By F. F. Bruce
5. We can be returned to a right relationship with God by accepting Jesus' sacrifice for our sins and letting it be known to others.
- • The Good News:
  - ○ "If you confess with your mouth, 'Jesus is Lord,' and believe in your heart that God raised him from the dead, you will be saved."[9]
  - ○ See also: Zechariah 13:9; Matthew 6:33; 7:7–8; Romans 5:1; 8:1, 38–39; and 2 Peter 3:9.
- • Books:
  - ○ "Why I Have Made Jesus Christ Lord of My Life" in *Why I Am a Christian* edited by Paul Hoffman and Norman Geisler
  - ○ *Live to Tell* by Brad Kallenberg
  - ○ *The Sacred Romance* by Brent Curtis and John Eldredge
  - ○ *Peace With God* by Billy Graham

HOW TO NAVIGATE WAYPOINT 11

At Waypoint 11, the traveler is growing in knowledge and has an increasingly positive attitude toward this good news. There will naturally be a growing understanding that God has a plan for his or her life, that God will empower him or her to have a better future.

11

POSITIVE ATTITUDE TOWARD THE GOOD NEWS

An emerging optimism and trust in the good news begins to grow within the traveler.

◈ 11-A ▷ God Wants to Empower Your Strengths

By supernaturally empowering certain strengths of the traveler, God creates spiritual gifts so the traveler can better serve others. The Bible states, "God's various gifts are handed out everywhere; but they all originate in God's Spirit. . . . God himself is behind it all. Each person is given something to do that shows who God is: Everyone gets in on it, everyone benefits. . . . The variety is wonderful."[10]

Spiritual Gifts

The Bible describes a variety of God-given gifts.[11] Here is a list of those Oksana observed in Francine:[12]

1. Encouragement: to comfort, console, encourage, and counsel.[13]
2. Faith: Understanding the purposes of God.[14]
3. Hospitality: Offering comfort and help to those in need.[15]
4. Mercy: To feel sympathy and compassion (accompanied by action) that mirrors Christ's love and alleviates suffering.[16]
5. Giving: Cheerfully giving of resources without regret.[17]
6. Prayer: Passionate, extended, and effective prayer.[18]
7. Helping: Empowering others to increase their service to the needy.[19]
8. Teaching: Communicating difficult concepts in a clear and relevant way that results in learning.[20]
9. Bearing good news (sometimes called evangelism): Building relationships that help travelers move toward a personal knowledge and experience with God.[21]

Oksana learned of these gifts mostly through Francine's example. Yet, it made such an impression on Oksana that she began to wonder if God could help her overcome her abusive flare-ups. "How can I be strong like you?" Oksana asked one evening. "God gives his power to those who serve others in his name," was Francine's simple, confident reply.[22]

◈ 11-B ▷ God Wants to Help You Overcome Weaknesses

For all of her fascination about how God could foster her strengths, it was Oksana's weaknesses that bothered her the most. Yet here was more good news. Francine explained, in her sometimes awkward translations, that God had a plan to help everyone overcome personal weaknesses. In fact, Francine herself had been the recipient of such help, and now felt she had permanently left behind her own abusive tendencies.

Bible passages that Francine translated included the following:

- "Don't panic. I'm with you. There's no need to fear for I'm your God. I'll give you strength. I'll help you. I'll hold you steady, keep a firm grip on you."[23]
- "Is anyone crying for help? God is listening, ready to rescue you."[24]
- "And do not set your heart on what you will eat or drink; do not worry about it. For the pagan world runs after all such things, and your Father knows that you need them. But seek his kingdom, and these things will be given to you as well."[25]
- "I can do everything through him who gives me strength"[26]
- "Don't you realize that this is not the way to live? Unjust people who don't care about God will not be joining in his kingdom. Those who use and abuse each other, use and abuse sex, use and abuse the earth and everything in it, don't qualify as citizens in God's kingdom. A number of you know from experience what I'm talking about, for not so long ago you were on that list. Since then, you've been cleaned up and given a fresh start by Jesus, our Master, our Messiah, and by our God present in us, the Spirit."[27]

It was this last passage that hit Oksana especially hard. "Those who use and abuse each other . . ." that described Oksana exactly. And that had driven Arjan away.

QUESTIONS FOR PERSONAL REFLECTION

1. What are strengths you feel God has given you? How do you think he wants you to use these strengths to serve others?
2. What are weaknesses that you need to overcome?

PROBLEM

We were far too weak and rebellious to do
anything to get ourselves ready.

—Paul of Tarsus[1]

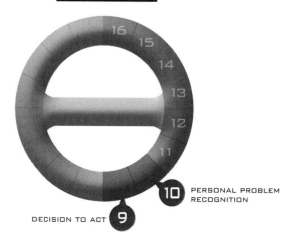

16
15
14
13
12
11

10 PERSONAL PROBLEM
RECOGNITION

DECISION TO ACT **9**

OUT OF THE BLEAK

It was September 11, 2001, and Oksana sat at a lunchroom table with her charges—seven little pre-schoolers, finally safe behind the walls of St. Jerome's church, far enough away from the horror. They now were silent, but tears still drew black streaks through the thick grey dust that had caked on their faces . . . including Oksana's. She gathered her seven charges closer in, whispering, "Come here. Come in." And they huddled as chicks beneath a mother hen's wings.

Oksana pulled up roots and moved to New York City. Her first ex, Jon, had moved with Jacob to Manhattan, and she had followed to be near her son. She found work at Trinity Episcopal Church dayschool in the heart of Manhattan and was beginning to settle in and thrive. Then today . . . life came crashing down around her.

They had heard it—the first tower, as it fell. Trinity Church was only blocks from the twin towers. As the foundations of the earth shook, and the sky went black, all Oksana could do was stumble along, dragging behind her the seven little preschoolers as they clung to each other's hands in a delicate chain, all of them following Reverend Stuart through the thick-dust fog. With her chicks in tow, Oksana tried to keep up with Stuart, but his lanky strides outpaced her. His black clerical shirt would disappear in the gray dust that settled about them all. Then he'd reappear, beckoning them onward.

This time, Oksana could not tell what happened to Stuart. She looked intently for him, but he was nowhere in sight. The pastor who had led them out of the billowing darkness was gone—maybe he'd gone back into the death and chaos. Though it appeared that all eighty of the day school students and all twenty of their attendants had survived the trek away from ground zero, Stuart still hadn't returned. Her spiritual guide was not there with her now when she needed him.

As the chaplain of Trinity Episcopal Church, he was her pastor. He was the one she had sought for guidance when she had failed miserably just a few weeks earlier . . . horribly. He knew her hope. And now where was he?

One by one, parents came stumbling toward their little cluster, some weeping, some screaming in hysterical joy, some in a silent daze; and they went away desperately clinging to each other. Then with the last child waving to her over her mother's shoulder, Oksana was alone—alone, and without Stuart.

"You've been through a lot, I can tell."

Oksana's hope returned as she looked up, and a clerical collar and a black shirt met her gaze. But even as she began to wonder how Stuart could have cleaned himself so quickly of the gray dust, her eyes fixed on a face that, though warm, was not Stuart's.

Henry was a priest at St. Jerome's Catholic Church; and over the next several hours, Oksana talked, and Henry listened. On occasions, he'd wipe some filth from her face, get her a drink of water, or hold her close as she unexplainably began to sob into his shoulder, smearing his neat black fabric with her gray grime.

She couldn't stop talking, and he wouldn't stop listening. He'd never met her before, yet he cared for her as though she were his daughter. He cared for her even when she began to reveal her recent failures at the day-care center—why she was on probation . . . how she had come to lose control and slap that child. Stuart had stood by her and had shown her forgiveness, and now she was confessing her struggles to Father Henry.

Though Henry was Catholic and Stuart was Episcopalian, she felt a strange comfort and commonality with both. It seemed as if Henry was carrying on for Stuart as her guide. "So your father hurt you. And when you can't handle things, you hurt others?" was Father Henry's summation.

At that, Oksana fell silent. She simply stared away at the door.

"Do you want God to give you power to change, Oksana?"

Her heart ached. She felt herself drawing away from him. "I've never seen God change anyone," was Oksana's quiet, yet firm reply.

She looked up at the priest's kind face—he just kept listening intently. But her old anger seethed out. "The only power I've seen from God is the power to hurt and lie. My father was a Christian one day a week and an abuser the rest. Did God give him that power?" Oksana's gaze fell back to the floor, but her voice was far more resolute now.

Far too long the room was silent, save for each of their breathing. Then softly came Father Henry's reply, "You've confused the two: your father and our Father." Oksana felt the tightness in her chest and throat as another sob crept up. She fought for control, shaking her head and clenching her fists. She fought that way for an eternal few minutes in silence.

And then she felt his hand rest upon her shoulder and gently pat. Low and gracious, his voice assured her, "Take some time, and let's talk more later. Let me introduce you to our Father."

Though the offer sounded hollow, with language reminiscent of the fake people of her church-going youth, the events and emotions of the past six hours had been too much for Oksana. She nodded. She had seen something in these men who helped her that day—something more patient, more kind, and more fatherly than she had ever known.

Oksana heard a disturbance of laughter, voices, and scattered clapping behind her. Father Henry's glance had broken away from her in that direction. And a great smile had broken across his face. Standing up, he called and beckoned.

"Reverend Stuart—over here!"

She turned to see her guide and friend. He was covered from head to toe in uniform gray dust, except for his broad smile and bright eyes.[2]

HOW TO NAVIGATE WAYPOINT 10

At Waypoint 10, travelers recognize a personal problem which they feel helpless to eliminate. The problem may be addiction, abuse, dishonesty, or a host of other ills. Two signposts can help the traveler navigate this problem.

> **10**
>
> **PERSONAL PROBLEM RECOGNITION**
>
> Here, travelers recognize a personal problem, one so challenging they are incapable of addressing it without God's help.

10-A YOU ARE NOT ALONE

Many times that day, the stalwart presence of both Stuart and Father Henry comforted Oksana and reminded her that she was not alone. But their strength seemed to come from somewhere else, somewhere other.

SOMEWHERE OTHER

- "When I said, 'My foot is slipping,' your love, O LORD, supported me. When anxiety was great within me, your consolation brought joy to my soul. . . . But the LORD has become my fortress, and my God the rock in whom I take refuge."[3]
- "He reached down from on high and took hold of me; he drew me out of deep waters. He rescued me from my powerful enemy, from my foes, who were too strong for me. They confronted me in the day of my disaster, but the LORD was my support."[4]
- "We call Abraham 'father' not because he got God's attention by living like a saint, but because God made something out of Abraham when he was a nobody. . . . When everything was hopeless, Abraham believed anyway . . . He plunged into the promise and came up strong, ready for God, sure that God would make good on what he had said."[5]

10-B THREE LANTERNS

Oksana's opinion about spiritual fathers began to slowly change over the next several months, as she weekly took the subway from her flat in Brooklyn to see Father Henry at St. Jerome's. Father Henry emphasized three concepts from the Bible that began to illuminate Oksana's spiritual path.

LANTERN 1. God is a loving heavenly Father who wants us to join his family.[6] Over the months of conversations that ensued, Father Henry did not try to rationalize or explain away either her earthly father's abuse or the tragedy of what was becoming known as 9/11. Instead, Father Henry introduced Oksana to a loving heavenly Father.

THE LOVING FATHER

- "What marvelous love the Father has extended to us! Just look at it—we're called children of God! That's who we really are. But that's also why the world doesn't recognize us or take us seriously, because it has no idea who he is or what he's up to."[7]
- "You can tell for sure that you are now fully adopted as his own children because God sent the Spirit of his Son into our lives crying out, 'Papa! Father!' Doesn't that privilege of intimate conversation with God make it plain that you are not a slave, but a child? And if you are a child, you're also an heir, with complete access to the inheritance."[8]

LANTERN 2. The heavenly Father has made himself known, in the person of Jesus Christ, his Son. The heavenly Father sent his Son to illuminate our journey and be our personal guide. Jesus Christ experienced every temptation humans experience, yet he did not give in to sin.[9] Oksana began to understand that the heavenly Father of the Bible was demonstrating that he had power over personal problems. She began to grasp that this heavenly Father, unlike her earthly father, could help with life's greatest struggles. To Oksana, this demonstrated a new kind of fatherhood: a loving, useful, and more-than-natural fatherhood.

LANTERN 3. The heavenly Father loves us, and sent his Son to lay down his life for all travelers. Oksana began to believe that though humans can't solve their problems, it made sense that God can. She saw that, as Stuart had been willing even to give his life. Jesus gave his life to die on our behalf—on her behalf. Oksana was mesmerized as Father Henry described the story of Jesus' death and resurrection—how God demonstrated once and for all that death was not the end of life's journey.

HOW TO NAVIGATE WAYPOINT 9

One of the most common feelings at Waypoint 9 is a sense of suspension between two lives, two worlds, and two destinies. At Trinity Church, Oksana felt called to a new life, but after emerging from the gritty haze

> **9**
> **DECISION TO ACT**
> The traveler makes a personal decision to reach out to God for help, forgiveness, and grace.

of her old life, she felt called backward, to retreat to the familiar roads of her past.

To navigate this waypoint, the traveler must heed three signposts that point the way forward: the gap, the one bridge, and the decision.

9-A THE GAP

There is a gap that separates humans from God. The gap exists because God is a perfect Father, and every traveler makes mistakes and falls short of the ideal God created us to be.[10] We may slap a child in a moment of frustration, or simply toss around careless but harmful words that strike deep into another's soul. Here are some Bible passages that emphasize the gap between people and God:

- "There's nothing wrong with God; the wrong is in you. Your wrongheaded lives caused the split between you and God. Your sins got between you so that he doesn't hear."[11]
- "If we claim that we're free of sin, we're only fooling ourselves. A claim like that is errant nonsense. On the other hand,

if we admit our sins—make a clean breast of them—he won't let us down; he'll be true to himself. He'll forgive our sins and purge us of all wrongdoing."[12]

- "For all have sinned and fall short of the glory of God."[13]

9-B THE ONE BRIDGE

The traveler must also understand that a loving heavenly Father has built a bridge to span the gap between him and us:

- "This is how much God loved the world: He gave his Son, his one and only Son. And this is why: so that no one need be destroyed; by believing in him, anyone can have a whole and lasting life."[14]

- "Since we've compiled this long and sorry record as sinners (both us and them) and proved that we are utterly incapable of living the glorious lives God wills for us, God did it for us. Out of sheer generosity he put us in right standing with himself. A pure gift. He got us out of the mess we're in and restored us to where he always wanted us to be. And he did it by means of Jesus Christ."[15]

- "But God demonstrates his own love for us in this: While we were still sinners, Christ died for us."[16]

- "But God's gift is real life, eternal life, delivered by Jesus, our Master."[17]

- "But we see Jesus, who was made a little lower than the angels, now crowned with glory and honor because he suffered death, so that by the grace of God he might taste death for everyone. In bringing many sons to glory, it was fitting that God, for whom and through whom everything exists, should make the author of their salvation perfect through suffering. Both the one who makes men holy and those who are made holy are of the same family. So Jesus is not ashamed to call them brothers."[18]

Sometimes travelers wonder if another bridge spans the gap. They wonder if perhaps Buddha, Mohammed, or Shiva has built a bridge. Yet while other religions may claim to have spanned the chasm, Jesus clearly states that only through him does the bridge to God exist:

- "Jesus answered, 'I am the way and the truth and the life. No one comes to the Father except through me.'"[19]
- One Bible translation adds traveler imagery: "Jesus said, 'I am the Road, also the Truth, also the Life. No one gets to the Father apart from me. If you really knew me, you would know my Father as well. From now on, you do know him. You've even seen him!'"[20]

9-C IT'S YOUR DECISION

To many, it can seem easier to stand on the edge of the gap and peer at the future from afar, but the Bible emphasizes that one must make a decision if one wants God's help. He won't force his help upon anyone.

- "But if serving the LORD seems undesirable to you, then choose for yourselves this day whom you will serve . . . But as for me and my household, we will serve the LORD."[21]
- "Here I am! I stand at the door and knock. If anyone hears my voice and opens the door, I will come in and eat with him, and he with me."[22]
- "Everyone who calls on the name of the Lord will be saved."[23]
- "Yet to all who received him, to those who believed in his name, he gave the right to become children of God."[24]
- To the young businessman, Jesus replied, "First things first. Your business is life, not death. Follow me. Pursue life."[25]

Finally, Oksana found herself confronting the questions that were at the root of this faith: Where do you stand? On which side of the gap are you? Will you cross the bridge?

As Father Henry insisted, "The joy of travel lies in moving, not staying put."

Questions for Personal Reflection

1. How do you feel when comparing yourself to an all-powerful heavenly Father?
2. What in your past has made you feel separated and unable to live up to God's expectations?

BIRTH

But God put his love on the line for us by offering his Son in sacrificial death while we were of no use whatever to him.

—Paul of Tarsus[1]

NEW BIRTH **7**

8 REPENTANCE AND FAITH IN CHRIST

INDIAN POINT

The trip from Springfield was much shorter than she remembered as a child. But soon it appeared up ahead: Indian Point. This was a grove of oak trees perched high upon a bluff overlooking Indian Creek. This was not far from here where Oksana grew up, and it was where her family had attended church. *How strange, yet familiar*, she thought. After all of these years, she was traveling back to Illinois—to Indian Point Church. Oksana could not explain the feelings, nor the tug to return to the church of her youth. But here she was, headed back on the afternoon of Thanksgiving.

A year had passed since those fateful days of 9/11, and as New York irrevocably changed, so had Oksana. Something about the horrific events, the fearless guidance of Stuart, and most of all the weekly meetings with Father Henry, had stabilized her life. She had settled well into her position at the day school at Trinity Church. It was in this capacity that she had headed back to the Midwest to attend a conference in Springfield. With the Thanksgiving holiday approaching and no family left in the Midwest, Oksana decided to remain the few days until Thanksgiving and travel the roads of her Midwestern roots. It was then that she decided to visit Indian Point Church on Thanksgiving Day, not knowing what she might find.

Indian Point is an ancient outcropping in the green valleys north of Springfield. As the highway runs north along Indian Creek, eventually Indian Point comes into view. Almost two hundred feet higher than the surrounding landscape and topped with a grove of ancient oaks, Indian Point juts out above the road like the prow of a magnificent ship. *Little wonder*, Oksana thought, *that the First Nations People would build their village on its crest.*

Now all that remained was a church, some one hundred and fifty years old with English Georgian architecture. As she pulled the rental car onto the side road and began the ascent to the church, the trees and hedgerows filled her with memories of her youth. To her surprise, a half dozen cars were in the small lot adjacent to the church, and an older couple was entering. Instinctively perhaps, Oksana parked the car and headed up an overgrown footway to the church stopping only once to take a picture, which she would later glue in her waypoint journal.

Indian Point Church
Athens, Illinois[2]

It was just as she remembered. Nothing had changed except the faces. The little church held no more than fifty people, and today a dozen or so were gathered. The service had started, and though several attendees glanced at Oksana and one nodded sociably, no one spoke to her.

"I guess we'll start with the sermon," came the announcement from an elderly gentleman with a faded red shirt and frayed black coat. "If Erie can't get here to play the organ, then I guess a sermon's all we got." With that, a low chuckle arose from the audience, and though Oksana could not recall the faces, the atmosphere was familiar.

The man in the faded coat was Martin, a farmer; he and Louise, his wife, had followed his parents in attending this church. Oksana guessed she must have known them from years ago, but try as she may, she could not remember. "The sermon is the only one I can give," began Martin. "And, I guess it's only on Thanksgiving that you have to hear me give it. But it's my story." And so began Martin's account of his spiritual journey.

Martin's story was of a GI returning from the Korean Conflict. "I was headstrong, full of myself," recalled Martin, "but I was also out of control." Martin described a life of alcohol-fueled failures: failure at employment, failure at home, and failure at marriage. "I realized I had to make a choice, but I didn't think I had the power. And then I met Louise, and she became my second wife. She showed me it was Christ who could give me that power. But, she said it was more than just believing. I had to live differently too. I didn't think of God that way— someone who could still do miracles. But I asked him to do one. And I guess he did." To which a muffled "amen" came from the direction of Louise, and to which a chuckle erupted from the audience.

After the service, the aloofness of the congregation dissipated and Oksana was engulfed in a tide of well wishers. The deluge intensified when they heard that she had grown up in the church, with some offering unsettling stories of Oksana's parents. Eventually, the crowd dispersed, and in the parking lot, Louise invited Oksana to their home.

Oksana wanted to go desperately, but the awkward discussions about her father made her feel uncomfortable. Reluctantly, she declined and headed back to Springfield, later writing in her journal:

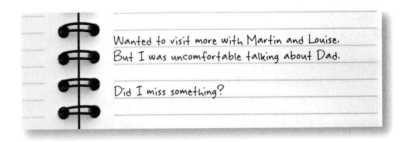

Wanted to visit more with Martin and Louise.
But I was uncomfortable talking about Dad.

Did I miss something?

SIMMER

That winter, back in New York was an especially difficult one for Oksana. She had almost no contact with Jacob. Jon continued to fight to keep Oksana away because of her abusive history. Though Oksana had not hit, nor even raised her voice in anger against a child in over a year, many still thought that it was too soon to fully trust her.

As spring arrived in New York City, and the bitter chill was replaced with the sun peeking through the stone canyons, Oksana yearned once again for the bluffs and fields of central Illinois. With the day school's Easter vacation approaching, Oksana planned to return to Illinois and Indian Point.

It was on Easter Sunday that Oksana returned to that ancient outcropping. Though she knew it was not likely, she hoped to hear Martin speak once more his plain stories of life. The church was noticeably fuller than during her last visit, but now a young seminary student replaced Martin in delivering the message. The seminarian gave a hearty attempt, but Oksana found his message too complicated to follow. So, she daydreamed, looking about the sanctuary that held so many memories. And then she spied her. It was Louise, now at the far side of the front pew. But she looked older, years older.

After the service, Oksana approached Louise to perhaps take her up on the invitation for lunch. "Do you remember me?" began Oksana. At first puzzled, Louise's face quickly turned to a welcoming smile as she embraced her. Over the next several hours, Louise and Oksana shared a small meal in Louise's room at a nursing home in Athens. Oksana learned that Martin had passed away early in January, and Louise was unable to hold onto the farm. She had moved into a nursing home and was making new friends, but Louise missed Martin's vigorous energy and full-bodied laugh. Finally, Oksana broached the reason for her visit.

"Your husband said some things I wanted to ask him about," Oksana said, no longer able to hold back her questions and search for clarification.

"He talked about God helping him overcome problems, about a miracle. About how he had to do more than believe; he had to let people know why." Louise replied with a demure grin, "And who told him those things?"

Over the next several hours Louise gave Oksana three insights that brought Martin's observations into perspective. Oksana wrote them down in her waypoint journal this way:

Louise said:
1. I must be truly sorry and make a mental decision to break with my past. This is called "repentance."[3]

2. I have to trust God, and he will give me the power to change. This is called "faith."[4]

3. Then God can turn me around, change my mind about things. It may mean allowing God to make a complete change in my way of life. This is "conversion."[5]

The terms brought up distasteful memories from their misuse in Oksana's youth, but on Louise's lips, they sounded fresh, even exhilarating. And it was this last element that intrigued Oksana the most: "allowing God to make a complete change in my way of life."

MATRIX

Returning to New York City, Oksana renewed her weekly meetings with Father Henry. And she began to recall her earlier meetings with Stuart. In both of these encounters, she observed how each came to follow Christ. She found they had different journeys from Martin's, but with a similar result.

Father Henry described how he had decided to enter the priesthood after a mysterious and supernatural encounter as a teenager. Coming from a wealthy family, he had all the money and friends that should make a young man happy. But he still felt empty. It was after a stormy night when a tornado devastated nearby homes that Father Henry had what he called "an encounter" at the next day's mass. The Communion somehow seemed different to him, the incense somehow stronger, and the prayers somehow directed at him.

Unable to resist what he sensed was a magnificent call, he lingered afterwards to talk to Sister Faustina. It was then that he decided to ask God to help him change and give him power to serve others. And he sensed that in this mysterious encounter, God was calling him and empowering him for what lay ahead. "Our sacramental tradition teaches us that Catholic evangelism always involves the 'acceptance of signs,' as Pope Paul VI put it," said Father Henry.[6] "I haven't looked back since."

Stuart's decision could not have been more different; he grew up in a religious family. "I could not recall a time when I was not a Christian," Stuart had recounted. "Some people have a sordid past. I never did. I was just shy. Sometimes I was intolerably shy. But as I became a teen, I started to realize that withdrawing was selfish. I withdrew because it made me feel better. It was all about me. I knew in my heart it was a failure. And though I felt inadequate, very inadequate, I asked God to give me power to change and make other people my priority."

Shy was not a word Oksana would have ever have used to describe Stuart, yet somehow it fit. He had been commanding when needed, gentle when warranted, and always sensitive to others. She could still hear his words ringing in her memory. "Maybe God took my self-centered shyness and made a new Stuart, one that could serve him better. Everyone who knew me growing up thinks it is a miracle."

HOW TO NAVIGATE WAYPOINT 8

8

REPENTENCE AND FAITH IN CHRIST

Travelers recognize they have not lived up to God's standards, and that only by faith in Christ Jesus and his death on their behalf, can they escape the penalty.

Oksana has encountered Waypoint 8. It is a place where travellers realize that they need to go in another direction: They are genuinely sorry for their wrongs; they sense God can provide the power to change; and they prepare to act. That is what happened to Oksana.

Through the stories of Martin, Father Henry, and Stuart, Oksana saw that she would be unable to change by herself because she had a deep-seated problem. She needed help. It was in their stories that Oksana began to understand that God grants power to those who will follow.

And yet, there was a dead end, a blind alley up ahead with no outlet on her spiritual journey. Oksana avoided it, but to help other travelers avoid it as well, it bears mentioning: it is the dead end of believing, not following.

THE DEAD END

Many people feel that mere belief in God is all that is required to go to heaven. Living a changed life often seems optional. But as Oksana continued her conversations with Louise and Father Henry, she began to understand that God requires holy living as well.[7] Scriptures that underscore this include the following:

- "As obedient children, let yourselves be pulled into a way of life shaped by God's life, a life energetic and blazing with holiness. God said, 'I am holy; you be holy.'"[8]
- "For physical training is of some value, but godliness has value for all things, holding promise for both the present life and the life to come."[9]
- "Submit yourselves, then, to God. Resist the devil, and he will flee from you. Come near to God and he will come near to you.

Wash your hands, you sinners, and purify your hearts, you double-minded. Grieve, mourn and wail. Change your laughter to mourning and your joy to gloom. Humble yourselves before the Lord, and he will lift you up."[10]

- "What is required is serious obedience—doing what my Father wills. I can see it now—at the Final Judgment thousands strutting up to me and saying, 'Master, we preached the Message, we bashed the demons, our God-sponsored projects had everyone talking.' And do you know what I am going to say? 'You missed the boat. All you did was use me to make yourselves important. You don't impress me one bit. You're out of here.'"[11]

8-A EXPECT THE SUPERNATURAL

As the stories of Martin, Father Henry, and Stuart unfolded, Oksana began to see a supernatural intersection at the heart of this change:[12]

- "For it is by grace you have been saved, through faith—and this not from yourselves, it is the gift of God—not by works, so that no one can boast. For we are God's workmanship."[13]

- Another translation paraphrases this passage, making God's participation abundantly clear: "Saving is all his idea, and all his work. All we do is trust him enough to let him do it. It's God's gift from start to finish! We don't play the major role. If we did, we'd probably go around bragging that we'd done the whole thing! No, we neither make nor save ourselves. God does both the making and saving. He creates each of us by Christ Jesus to join him in the work he does, the good work he has gotten ready for us to do, work we had better be doing."[14]

8-B THE CHOICE IS YOURS

In each of the connections with Martin, Father Henry, and Stuart, it was evident to Oksana that travelers have free will. God may beckon them, but they have the choice of what road they will travel.[15]

8-C ▸ DECLARE IT VERBALLY AND IN ACTION

Two more signposts came into view as the stories of Martin, Father Henry, and Stuart came together. Oksana wrote the following in her waypoint journal, adding Scriptures and paraphrasing what she learned.

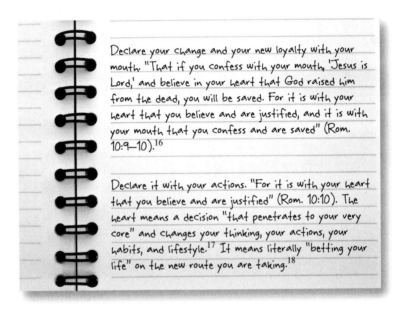

Declare your change and your new loyalty with your mouth. "That if you confess with your mouth, 'Jesus is Lord,' and believe in your heart that God raised him from the dead, you will be saved. For it is with your heart that you believe and are justified, and it is with your mouth that you confess and are saved" (Rom. 10:9–10).[16]

Declare it with your actions. "For it is with your heart that you believe and are justified" (Rom. 10:10). The heart means a decision "that penetrates to your very core" and changes your thinking, your actions, your habits, and lifestyle.[17] It means literally "betting your life" on the new route you are taking.[18]

OKSANA'S EXPERIENCE AT WAYPOINT 7

Waypoint 7 was now on Oksana's horizon. It may be the most important and misunderstood encounter on the journey.[19] It is the point at which the natural and mystical collide most forcefully and surprisingly.

At Waypoint 7, travelers ask for forgiveness for their failings, they trust in God to forgive and change them, after which God supernaturally gives them power to begin a new journey of serving others. Here is how Jesus describes it: "So don't be so surprised when I tell you that you have to be 'born from above'—out of this world, so to speak. You know well enough how the wind blows this way and that. You hear it rustling through the trees, but you have no idea where it comes from or where it's headed next. That's the way it is with everyone 'born from above' by the wind of God, the Spirit of God."[20]

LOOK AT IT

Louise had just finished describing the circumstances of her youthful marriage when Oksana blurted out, "Did Martin really change? I mean, how did you know something actually happened? Did he look different?"

"He may have looked different to God," came Louise's soft reply. "But no, he didn't look different to me. At not least right away. You see, Martin was in the back forty acres for most of one evening. He told me he was watching the sun go down, and that God spoke to him there. He said he never felt closer to God. He was so embarrassed by his failings. But he said God knew them. And though he was embarrassed, he felt God still loved him. He felt like he had come home, like after the war, and he was totally loved and accepted by his heavenly Father. He was home, where he was always supposed to be."

The words *home where he was supposed to be* continued to haunt Oksana that summer in New York. And it was another holiday, July 4, when the day school was closed and Oksana had a day off, that she found herself wandering the Brooklyn Heights area. She had intended to take the pedestrian walkway across the Brooklyn Bridge to see the tall sailing ships on the East River. But on her way to the bridge, she passed a church whose architecture in some ways reminded her of the Indian Point church. The name of this Brooklyn church seemed appropriate to her quest: Plymouth Church of the Pilgrims.

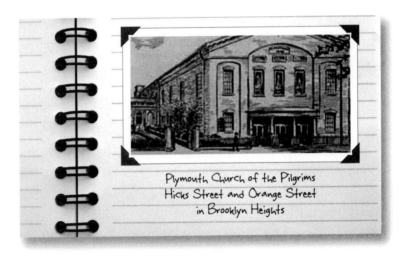

Plymouth Church of the Pilgrims
Hicks Street and Orange Street
in Brooklyn Heights

WIND

Oksana didn't know of this church's prominent history protecting slaves on their journey to freedom on the Underground Railroad. Nor did she know about their first pastor, Henry Ward Beecher, whose powerful preaching and outspoken opposition to slavery filled the pews to overflowing.[21]

Oksana just felt a sense of safety. In the muted light of an empty sanctuary, she found a haven and who she was seeking. Oksana never told anyone what she encountered in that place of refuge. But Oksana did not emerge the same.

She would later write in her waypoint journal:

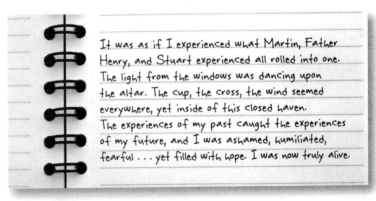

It was as if I experienced what Martin, Father
Henry, and Stuart experienced all rolled into one.
The light from the windows was dancing upon
the altar. The cup, the cross, the wind seemed
everywhere, yet inside of this closed haven.
The experiences of my past caught the experiences
of my future, and I was ashamed, humiliated,
fearful . . . yet filled with hope. I was now truly alive.

HOW TO NAVIGATE WAYPOINT 7

 7-A IT IS NORMAL TO FEEL ASHAMED (REPENTANCE)

Those who encounter Waypoint 7 experience an inner, mental decision to make a break with their past. Memories of the past are being replaced by visions of what an ideal future with God can look like. The traveler will often be wavering between anticipation (of the future) and guilt (over the past). This is normal, for God is showing how his design for the future is so much better than one's past.

> **7**
>
> NEW BIRTH
> God creates an intersection between the spiritual and physical worlds, and a new person is born.

The Scriptures say, "And what we see is that anyone united with the Messiah gets a fresh start, is created new. The old life is gone; a new life [begins]! Look at it!"[22]

7-B IT IS NORMAL TO FEEL UNINFORMED ABOUT GOD (GROWING IN FAITH)

At Waypoint 7, travelers are growing with an inner confidence and knowledge of God. They may be curious, confused, and even befuddled because they are gaining a clearer picture of where their route with God will take them.

Travelers should read God's promises first-hand. Get a good, readable Bible. There are many translations, but *The Message*, *The Living Bible*, and *The Good News Bible* are some good places to start.

THREE WAYS TO GET A FREE BIBLE
WITHOUT STEALING IT FROM A HOTEL

1. Take it! Actually, the Gideons who put the Bibles in the hotel rooms want you take them. So go ahead; Take it.

2. You can get a free copy of the Bible by visiting almost any local church.

3. You can find the entire *The Message* Bible online at http://www.Bible Gateway.com and http://www.americanbible.org/bible-resources. And you can find Bible passages to help with most of life's most pressing problems at http://www.gideons.org/readthebible/helps.aspx.

 7-C IT IS NORMAL TO FEEL HELPLESS ABOUT CHANGING YOUR LIFE (CONVERSION)[23]

Travelers at Waypoint 7 are ready to experience a "turn around . . . a change of mind . . . (to turn) from something to something (else)."[24] This has been called conversion, but that is an awkward word. It is really better described as reversing direction and going the opposite way. But the traveler will usually feel inadequate about attempting this. After all, like Oksana, travelers have usually tried to do this themselves many times before.

But Waypoint 7 is different.[25] As noted earlier, it is an intersection of the natural with the supernatural. New fortitude, confidence, and power well up inside the traveler, not like previous human attempts. This help is from a divine source. Oksana began to see that this source was the one who created her, loved her, willed his best for her, and who described himself as her heavenly Father. Father Henry's admonition almost one year earlier had been prophetic when he said to Oksana, "Let me introduce you to our Father."

7-D ARE YOU READY TO CHANGE?[26]

Oksana penned the following prayer in her waypoint journal. In various forms, it has been the prayer of countless travelers. Oksana would return to it many times because it held a strength and power. It was Oksana's point of decision—her prayer of repentance, faith, and change.

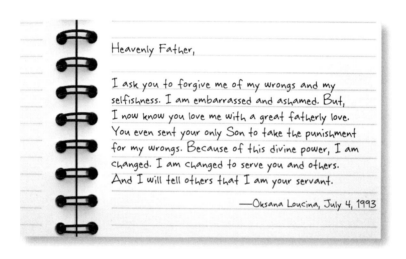

Heavenly Father,

I ask you to forgive me of my wrongs and my selfishness. I am embarrassed and ashamed. But, I now know you love me with a great fatherly love. You even sent your only Son to take the punishment for my wrongs. Because of this divine power, I am changed. I am changed to serve you and others. And I will tell others that I am your servant.

—Oksana Loucina, July 4, 1993

QUESTIONS FOR PERSONAL REFLECTION

1. "Let every detail in your lives—words, actions, whatever—be done in the name of the Master, Jesus."[27] What does this mean to you?
2. In your waypoint journal, write how you experienced Waypoints 8 and 7.
3. How have you declared your change in course? What were the circumstances? What were the outcomes? Was it important for you? Was it important for others?

LIFE

We need others. We need others to love and we need to be loved by them.
There is no doubt that without it, we too, like the infant left alone,
would cease to grow, cease to develop, choose madness and even death.

—Leo F. Buscaglia[1]

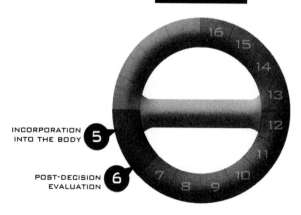

INCORPORATION
INTO THE BODY **5**

POST-DECISION
EVALUATION **6**

Two Communities

At last, thought Oksana, *I can see clearly!* The windows in her former apartment in Brooklyn were never so clean. And even though these windows looked upon a tenement high-rise, they could be windows cleaned from a small balcony. For Oksana this was the life she had always wanted: a new job as the director of a day school in Midtown Manhattan and a new apartment owned by the school. Clean and neat, this was the first time since living in Chicago that Oksana did not have a roommate; and the feeling of freedom, space, and spotlessness was a dream come true. In fact, since her decision seven months ago almost everything had seemed to improve. She now had money in the bank, a new apartment, a satisfying job, and a growing circle of friends.

It was with just such a bright outlook that she happily rushed to the door upon hearing the doorbell one Saturday morning. Many of the neighbors attended the church that owned her day school, and she was eager to make friends.

Upon opening the door, she found a heavyset man in a dark coat asked in a rasping low voice, "Oksana Loucina?"

"Yes," came her startled reply.

"This is for you," was the response. "You've been served." With that, the stranger quickly retreated with a parting "Sorry." And Oksana was left alone, sorting through several sheets of paper. The language confused her, but she understood the last line on the first page: "Do hereby sue the defendants, Oksana Loucina and the day school she serves, for 1.5 million dollars each."

Three days later in the office of the day school's lawyer, the news worsened. "They are suing us and you, Oksana," began Mark's explanation after a long look at the document. "They say you hit a child."

Oksana struggled to speak. She forced out the only words she could muster, "Why do this? It's not true."

"I've read the account you gave me, Oksana. And I believe you," replied Mark.

"But why do they say I did all this when I didn't?" Her voice grew more desperate.

"It's the lawyers. They are fishing, Oksana. When lawyers file a civil suit, they often go fishing by adding things you didn't do in hopes that when they investigate, you they will find some of these things. It's not based upon fact, it's based upon hunches."

"My job, my reputation, my son, Jacob?" came Oksana's reply in an increasingly faint tone.

"We will attend to those things after we defend this. There are people who know you, people who know that you didn't do it. We will get their sworn testimony, and the truth will come out."

More words were exchanged, but Oksana felt her mind disengaging—distancing from the room. Finally Mark rose to escort her out. "I've never thought that exaggerating charges did any good except to throw mud on everyone."

Mark's farewell was unsettling.

Oksana's walk across Midtown that January night was cold and slow. She had been astonished that so much had happened so fast. After she emerged last July from Plymouth Church of the Pilgrims, Oksana had been as free as a bird. She sang quietly on the subway. She helped out at a food kitchen two blocks from her apartment every Sunday. She improved in her relations with fellow employees at Trinity's day school. And when a new day school opened in Midtown operated by another church, Stuart had recommended her to be its director.

With a new job came new responsibilities, but also new friends, a new apartment, and a new life—a life where everyone related to Oksana, not according to her past, but based on whom she had become.

Now as she walked home from Mark's office, she looked back and wondered, *Those days were the best days I've ever known. Will they return?*

When Oksana finally made her way to her apartment, she took her waypoint journal from her bed stand and wrote:

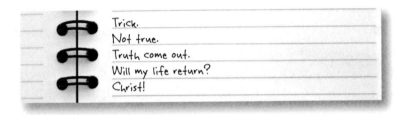

Trick.
Not true.
Truth come out.
Will my life return?
Christ!

CRUEL EDGES OF THE WORLD

Sunday approached, but Oksana stayed in her apartment. The phone rang several times, but she felt too uncertain to answer it. Feeling a little better on Monday morning, she prepared to go to work, though she was unsure how she would be received. It was while finishing her hair that a she heard a faint knock at the door. Wondering why someone would not ring the doorbell and instead tap so gently, she opened the door to find Francine.

Francine had moved to New York City from Chicago two years after Oksana. They had kept in touch since that first meeting on Chicago's Michigan Avenue. But now, after Oksana's decision to follow Christ, they had become even closer. Oksana even asked Francine to accompany her to the church that owned the day school. And soon the two became faithful attendees.

"You're not going to work," were the first words out of Francine's mouth. "We need to talk." Francine pushed past Oksana and entered the apartment.

Oksana followed, pulling the door closed behind. "Francine—not now. I have to go to work."

Francine turned back, sadly shaking her head. "No you don't, dear."

Over the next several hours, Oksana and Francine shared coffee. Francine had known the accusing child's mother since they first began attending the church. And Francine had already observed how the woman had become emotionally detached. Then when Oksana didn't show at church on Sunday and wouldn't answer her phone, Francine had been contacted and asked to "see how Oksana is doing" as well as apprise her that she shouldn't come in to work that day.

Oksana recounted how the nine-year-old boy had accused her of slapping him, not once but three times, when he dawdled too long on the playground.

"I raised my voice," insisted Oksana. "I was frustrated, but as I stand here before God, I did not hit him."

Francined assured her. "I know you've changed from the girl years ago on Michigan Avenue. I've seen how you've grown." Oksana shook her head and glanced away, a tear streaming down her cheek. Francine continued, "The church is afraid of the lawsuit. They won't listen right now." She reached up to Oksana's face with a tissue and wiped her cheeks.

Oksana rolled her eyes. "Sued for 1.5 million dollars? They don't have the money. They think that if they abandon me, the lawsuit will go away. It won't go away."

Francine smiled. "And neither will I," she insisted, grasping Oksana's hand.

As Oksana thought back upon the last seven months, nothing could have prepared her for such startling changes: a new life, new hopes, a prestigious job, a nice apartment, and new friends; but now lies, accusations, humiliation, and devastation.

Why would Jesus allow this to happen to me? Oksana's mind kept protesting. But her heart whispered, *He is always with you.*

How to Navigate Waypoint 6

6-A THE COSTS OF FOLLOWING CHRIST

A journey with Christ will not only be rewarding, but also challenging. God does not promise only ease for those who follow him. There will still be trials. This is how the Scriptures state it:

6

POST-DECISION EVALUATION

Here, the traveler reviews what has happened and whether the decision is worth the effort for the emerging criticism.

- "Mark my words, no one who sacrifices house, brothers, sisters, mother, father, children, land—whatever—because of me and the Message will lose out. They'll get it all back, but multiplied many times in homes, brothers, sisters, mothers, children, and land—but also in troubles."[2]
- "Even my best friend, the one I always told everything—he ate meals at my house all the time!—has bitten my hand. God, give grace, get me up on my feet."[3]
- "There are so many more . . . Through acts of faith, they toppled kingdoms, made justice work . . . Others braved abuse and whips, and, yes, chains and dungeons. We have stories of those who were stoned, sawed in two, murdered in cold blood; stories of vagrants wandering the earth in animal skins, homeless, friendless, powerless—the world didn't deserve them!—making their way as best they could on the cruel edges of the world."[4]
- "Bless those who persecute you; bless and do not curse."[5]
- "Do not repay anyone evil for evil. Be careful to do what is right in the eyes of everybody."[6]

Billy Graham tells of how, after his childhood conversion, he was immediately ridiculed at school. "'I understand we have Preacher Graham with us today,' one of my teachers said to the class some days later," Graham recalled. "Everybody laughed. She was making fun of me, and I felt some resentment. Then I remembered what Dr. Ham had said: when we come to Christ, we're going to suffer persecution."[7] That early encounter led Billy Graham to make a post-decision evaluation to follow Christ regardless of the cost.

6-B THE REWARDS OF FOLLOWING CHRIST

Though there are costs, the rewards are greater. The Scriptures say:

- "So we're not giving up. How could we! Even though on the outside it often looks like things are falling apart on us, on the inside, where God is making new life, not a day goes by without his unfolding grace. These hard times are small potatoes compared to the coming good times . . . The things we see now are here today, gone tomorrow. But the things we can't see now will last forever."[8]
- "'For I know the plans I have for you,' declares the LORD, 'plans to prosper you and not to harm you, plans to give you hope and a future.'"[9]
- "We've been given a glimpse of the real thing, our true home, our resurrection bodies! The Spirit of God whets our appetite by giving us a taste of what's ahead. He puts a little of heaven in our hearts so that we'll never settle for less."[10]

6-C THERE IS HELP

Because of the costs of following Christ, it is at Waypoint 6 that almost every traveler has second thoughts about continuing his or her journey. But, there is help. The Scriptures remind us:

- "God is our refuge and strength, an ever-present help in trouble."[11]
- "Stalwart [a person] walks in step with God; his path blazed by

God, he's happy. If he stumbles, he's not down for long; God has a grip on his hand."[12]

- "First pay attention to me, and then relax. Now you can take it easy—you're in good hands."[13]
- "I [Jesus] have told you these things, so that in me you may have peace. In this world you will have trouble. But take heart! I have overcome the world."[14]

OKSANA'S EXPERIENCE AT WAYPOINT 5

Caught in limbo between trust and suspicion, Oksana was fired.

She eventually found a job with Francine as a cleaner in a Manhattan department store. Her neat and tidy little world was replaced by a mattress on the floor of Francine's kitchen. Both ended their fellowship with the uptown church, making their way alone as best they could.

It was a sunny, spring morning and Oksana was rushing to her Sunday morning coffee with Francine. Francine and Oksana worked opposite shifts and this twice-weekly coffee was one of the few times they could meet. Today, Oksana was late and she rushed along West 76th Street toward Broadway.

She never saw the large sandwich board, the type that advertise daily specials along New York streets, until she was on top of it. It was too far into the pedestrian walkway, and she tumbled right over it, falling to the ground.

She heard people gasp, calling out, "Oh my," and "Are you OK?" But all she could focus on was her torn stocking, the last good pair she owned . . . and blood oozing from a rather nasty cut on her leg. She yelled a curse to no one in particular. A young man nearby stooped down and replied apologetically, "That's my sign. I'm sorry, it shouldn't be there. Let me help."

She opened her eyes to see a youngish man's face, wide-eyed and concerned. Beyond him, she caught sight of the offending sign, on its side and bent awkwardly: Journey Church. She couldn't help but think to herself, *How ironic.*

Nelson, the owner of the sign, helped Oksana into the foyer of what was an old church that had been converted to an off-Broadway theatre but was still used as a church on Sundays. It was musty, and the air was stale. Nelson hurriedly explained, "Don't worry. This is a church. I'm a pastor. Hard to believe, I know."

Nelson looked nothing like the pastors Oksana had known. He did not wear a clerical collar like Stuart or Father Henry, or even a coat and tie like Martin. He wore a casual shirt, untucked, and blue jeans. "If you'll let me, I'd like somebody from our church to take a look at that cut. We just want to help."

Oksana was too tired, embarrassed, and befuddled to refuse. She nodded, and Nelson ushered her from the foyer into the auditorium. A church service had started and there seemed to be some concern that Nelson was just arriving.

"Nelson—the service is starting," insisted a young man, reaching for him and motioning toward the front of an auditorium filled with more young people.

"She needs our help. Attend to her first," were Nelson's last words as he disappeared into the mass of people.

He was replaced at Oksana's side by Sue. "Let me look at that, I'm a nurse." And so arrived another companion on Oksana's journey.

Oksana enjoyed the morning service, almost to the point of forgetting the throbbing in her leg. The songs reminded her of the church with the day school, the magnificent auditorium reminded her of Trinity, and the gracious congregants reminded her of the people at Indian Point. But something was different. Their focus was something entirely new.

"We believe our growth groups are key to traveling with Christ," explained Sue. She volunteered with the church to help oversee the church's growth groups. "They meet one night a week, and their purpose is to give people a place to share with friends," explained Sue.

"If I go, I need Francine to come too," Oksana replied, and the two agreed to meet at a small group that Thursday in an apartment near where she and Francine lived.

For Oksana, the week plodded along in its usual monotonous rhythm, until at last it was Thursday night. The apartment building was ten blocks away, but it was a cool spring evening, and Oksana and Francine elected to walk. They were just about to exit the building when Oksana stopped short, gazing in disbelief out the door.

"Oh my—it can't be."

Francine halted, pulling her hand back from the doorknob. She spied a tall dark man, smiling and waving through the window. She glanced inquiringly at Oksana.

"Arjan!"

HOW TO NAVIGATE WAYPOINT 5

5-A FIND A FAITH FAMILY (IN A SMALL GROUP)

Oksana had already forged a relationship with Francine. But slowly, both Oksana and Francine realized they needed more. They had seen how a Christian community can lapse into suspicion, gossip, and destruction. But they had also seen at St. Jerome's, Trinity and Indian Point how churches could provide a community of support. But Trinity seemed so big, St. Jerome's so upscale, and Indian Point was too far away. Among a small group of friends in the apartment of Sy and Jimmy, they would began to foster a new family, a family unlike all others they had encountered.

> **5**
>
> INCORPORATION INTO THE BODY OF CHRIST
>
> Travelers seek out a supportive body of Christians who can help them navigate the road ahead.

"When two of you get together on anything at all on earth and make a prayer of it, my Father in heaven goes into action. And when two or three of you are together because of me, you can be sure that I'll be there."[15]

A FAITH FAMILY IS THE BODY OF CHRIST. The Scriptures describe the community of faith as Christ's "body" on the earth.[16] In the Scriptures, the word *body* emphasizes the organic, connected, and growing character of a faith family.[17] The Bible says, "The way God designed our bodies is a model for understanding our lives together as a church: every part dependent on every other part . . . If one part hurts, every other part is involved in the hurt, and in the healing. If one part flourishes, every other part enters into the exuberance."[18]

A FAITH FAMILY BREAKS DOWN BARRIERS. A community of faith also creates friendships between people of different generations and ethnicities. The Scriptures say that in a faith family, older men and women can share their insights with younger people.[19] Today, extended families are often scattered, but a faith family can be a great place for people of different ages and ethnicities to connect and accept one another.[20]

BEWARE THE DEAD END: ATTENDING CHURCH IS NOT THE SAME AS FINDING A FAITH FAMILY. A traveler may ask, "Is attending a church service the same as finding a faith family?" The answer is no. Attending church is not the same as participating in the life, service, and responsibility of a community of faith.

- "In this way we [the community of faith] are like the various parts of a human body. Each part gets its meaning from the body as a whole, not the other way around. The body we're talking about is Christ's body of chosen people. Each of us finds our meaning and function as a part of his body."[21]
- "Each person is given something to do that shows who God is: Everyone gets in on it, everyone benefits."[22]
- "You are Christ's body—that's who you are! You must never forget this. Only as you accept your part of that body does your 'part' mean anything."[23]

Though attending church services for teaching, worship, and prayer is important, the community of faith is much more than mere attendance. The community of faith is an ongoing family of fellow travelers who undertake life's journey together. They rely upon one another to overcome obstacles, detours, and challenges on the journey of life.

5-B THE CHURCH IS NOT PERFECT

Many people avoid church today because of poor preaching, unfriendly people, music that is too old or too loud, or a variety of other reasons. But the traveler that is serious about moving forward on his or her journey will overcome these obstacles. The Scriptures say, "Let us not give up meeting together, as some are in the habit of doing, but let us encourage one another—and all the more as you see the Day approaching."[24]

5-C THE EXCITEMENT OF SERVING OTHERS

God has created the fellowship of the journey so travelers can serve others. And deep down inside, most travelers want to help others. God provides through the church an organization that can serve others, and he provides through the power to do it the Holy Spirit. The Scriptures say:

- "Real religion, the kind that passes muster before God the Father, is this: Reach out to the homeless and loveless in their plight, and guard against corruption from the godless world."[25]
- "Sitting down, Jesus called the Twelve and said, "If anyone wants to be first, he must be the very last, and the servant of all."[26]
- "Let your light shine before men, that they may see your good deeds and praise your Father in heaven."[27]

Another translation makes this passage even clearer, "Be generous with your lives. By opening up to others, you'll prompt people to open up with God, this generous Father in heaven."[28]

QUESTIONS FOR PERSONAL REFLECTION

1. Are you (or have you been) experiencing a post-decision evaluation?
2. Have you found your faith family? Describe your fellowship circumstances.

FOUNDATIONS

Your Christians are so unlike your Christ.
—Mohandas Gandhi[1]

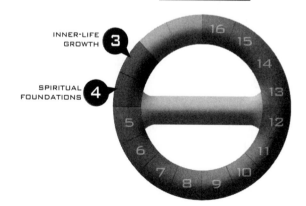

INNER-LIFE
GROWTH **3**

SPIRITUAL
FOUNDATIONS **4**

KITCHEN TALKS

Arjan had moved from Chicago months earlier in pursuit of a job opportunity. He knew he should be seeking out Oksana too, but it was . . . complicated. Then their mutual past found him out in the form of a subpoena. The authorities wanted to talk to him—about her.

Arjan and Oksana talked late into the night around Francine's kitchen table. Illuminated by only a small light, the shadows and Arjan's deep, resonante voice began to conjure memories long buried for Oksana. Arjan had always been her confidant in times of trouble. And he had been her guide as she struggled to remember those missing eleven years. Yet Arjan was so unlike her. She had grown to admire the tone of his skin and his long, flowing black hair, once she understood that Sikhs did not cut their hair but neatly rolled it up beneath a turban. Growing up in the Midwest, she had never met someone so different in appearance. Yet every time they spoke, she was drawn closer to a relationship that she knew must have been affectionate and faithful.

"So I won't testify Oksana," concluded Arjan at last. "I won't lie. I've seen you hit Jacob, and you've hit me too. If they ask me, I will be honest. So if I am going to help you, I can't testify."

"But then I'll lose Jacob," came Oksana's swift reply. "If you tell them that, they will never let me see Jacob again. Jon will keep him away from me forever. You don't want that do you, Arjan?"

Arjan had never liked Jon.

After Jon found Oksana lost among the Aboriginal rock paintings, she felt that she and Jon shared a destiny. But after they were married, Oksana grew impatient with Jon's long forays into the Outback with wealthy clients and their attractive wives. She had long suspected, but never been sure of Jon's infidelity. So, she found it absurd that Jon would break the news of such infidelity two weeks after she discovered she was pregnant. Her anger had been unrivaled that day. She had struggled with Jon, pulling a knife from his bush belt. The scar left on his upper arm seemed to bother him more than the invisible wound he left inside of her.

So it was little wonder when Jacob was born in Athens, Illinois, that Oksana did not tell her estranged husband. Still, Jon found out, and traveling to Springfield, he began a long legal battle to gain custody. Though he was awarded only partial custody, Jon renewed his efforts after the allegations at the day school—this time to gain sole custody.

"I couldn't bear not seeing Jacob again, Arjan," began Oksana's reply, slowly and quietly. "I've been worried all these years I would lose all rights to see him. And now because of their lies, I will. Oh please, please Arjan. You must lie too."

Arjan responded as he often did in such situations. He looked down at his hands. Oksana never knew if he was praying, thinking, or meditating, but slowly he rose and quietly passed through the apartment doorway and disappeared into the night. Oksana remained in her seat, watching him through the front window as he crossed the street in front of Francine's apartment. And she again was overtaken with a vague but overwhelming sense of loss.

In the subsequent weeks, Francine and Oksana made a point of attending Sy and Jimmy's growth group. In this small group, they developed deep and abiding friendships. Sy, a native New Yorker born in the Bowery, had worked his way up to an apartment in NoHo. Jimmy had been an art major at a Christian college in the Midwest, making his way to New York to open his own gallery. Corrie and Dave were college sweethearts from Indiana who sometimes volunteered as chefs for the church's many outreach events. And Wilbert was a confirmed bachelor who worked for the Metropolitan Transportation Authority. Sue, who Oksana first met when she patched up her gashed leg, rounded out this group.

Though they came from different locales and backgrounds, they all were united in their desire to grow in their knowledge of Jesus.

Jimmy was their teacher because he had three years of Bible courses in college, and no one else seemed to come close to this feat. And it was in Jimmy's gentle proddings that Oksana began to see that her journey would require her to shed more old baggage and to take some new journeys.

HOW TO NAVIGATE WAYPOINT 4

4

SPIRITUAL FOUNDATIONS

The traveler begins to grasp the essentials of what it means to follow Christ, how to live a godly life, and how to serve others.

Around the kitchen table of Sy and Jimmy's apartment, Oksana and her new found fellowship of travelers began to mature, expand, and grow in their understanding of what a life with Christ would be. *How remarkable*, she thought. *Jesus' teachings are nothing like I've thought. Or that I've seen. Jesus is so wise, so kind, so forgiving. I wish I was more like him.* The following are some of the foundations that Oksana learned from Jimmy in that apartment in NoHo.

4-A WHO JESUS IS

The gospel of Mark is a great place to start when learning about Jesus.[2] Read this gospel in your Bible and write down your thoughts in your waypoint journal.

JESUS IS A WISE TEACHER. The disciples discovered that Jesus was a great teacher, with powerful lessons about serving others.[3] But Jesus is more than a great teacher, as we shall see next.

JESUS IS A MIRACLE WORKER. At Waypoint 4, travelers begin to grasp that Jesus has power over the life-destroying effects of illness, addiction, harmful behaviors, behavioral disorders, and other negative situations.[4] But Jesus is even more than this.

JESUS IS GOD IN THE FLESH. It was easy then and today for people to believe that Jesus was just a great teacher. And it is somewhat easy to believe that he accomplished great miracles. Yet Jesus said he is more than this. He said that he is the Son of God—God in the flesh. It is important for the traveler to completely understand that Jesus is more than a great teacher and a miracle worker . . . Jesus is also God himself.[5]

JESUS' WORK. Jesus is the forgiver of sins, conqueror of death, and giver of the ultimate destination: eternal life.[6]

JESUS AND HIS WORKERS. Jesus sends followers out to carry his message to others.[7]

JESUS REQUIRES HOLY LIVING. Jesus also made it clear that following him includes living a life that models godly behavior and holy living.[8]

4-B YOU ARE BEING SPIRITUALLY SHAPED

After an understanding of who Jesus is, the traveler will start to be shaped into a healthy and godly spiritual life. But this does not come quickly. As a friend of mine likes to say, "Spiritual formation is a process, not a program. It cannot be packaged in a box, book, seminar, or special event."[9] It is a process of becoming more like Jesus in thinking and action. Here are four things travelers should keep in mind as they proceed onward:

1. Becoming more like Christ will continue throughout your life. Travelers with Jesus will never stop growing. There are still way-points ahead.

2. Becoming more like Christ means overcoming sins (wrong actions). Sin corrupts, but "if anyone is in Christ, he is a new creation; the old has gone, the new has come!"[10]

3. Becoming more like Christ is not the same as self-improvement. Self-improvement is often focused on a person's own standing, stature, or skills. But being more like Jesus means to serve others better, not yourself.[11]

4. Becoming more like Christ will have results. For example, the Scriptures describe the "fruit" of the Spirit, which travelers will develop.[12]

4-C EVERYTHING ABOUT YOU WILL GET SHAPED

God wants to take over everything and make all of you better: your head, heart, hands, and habits. This is sometimes called "holy living." And here is how Oksana, perhaps influenced in some manner by the Aboriginal rock paintings, pictured it in her waypoint journal.[13]

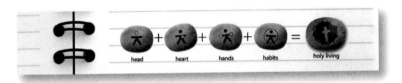

4-D SPIRITUAL SHAPING HAPPENS BEST IN SMALL GROUPS[14]

Ongoing, small fellowship groups, like the one around Sy and Jimmy's kitchen table, are the places where spiritual growth often takes place. Oksana would say later, "I got a lot from Nelson's sermons, but I got more from my small group." There are some important things to remember about small groups.

SMALL GROUPS ARE ONE OF THE BEST PLACES TO GROW YOUR SPIRITUAL FOUNDATIONS.[15] Look at Jesus' ministry. He drew twelve disciples to himself to mentor and then eventually to send out.[16]

SMALL GROUPS HAVE THREE TASKS THEY MUST UNDERTAKE TO BE HEALTHY. My friend Mike Breen led a church of twenty- and thirty-year-olds into becoming England's largest Anglican congregation.[17] The key was that everyone was in a healthy small group.[18] To keep these groups healthy, Breen emphasized that every small group must regularly do three things: reach *up*, reach *in*, and reach *out*. He used a triangle to help congregants maintain balance in these three essential aspects (see figure on page 97).

- UP: Every small group must have worship, Bible study, and prayer components where each attendee connects upward with God.

- IN: Every small group must have an inward component where the attendees build up one another through prayer, encouragement, and assistance.
- OUT: Every small group must be actively involved in reaching out and serving others.[19]

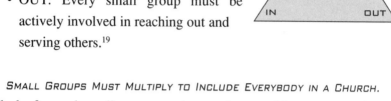

SMALL GROUPS MUST MULTIPLY TO INCLUDE EVERYBODY IN A CHURCH. A lack of enough small groups continues to be one of the most recurring weaknesses in churches today.[20] This is because almost every church has too few small groups. Thankfully for Oksana and Francine, Journey Church had plenty of small groups.

OKSANA'S EXPERIENCE AT WAYPOINT 3

Sy and Jimmy's apartment became the epicenter of Oksana's spiritual life. It was here that she weekly returned to share her successes and challenges. It was here that she felt truly accepted and able to open up about her most personal hopes and doubts. It was here that she finally wrestled with her fear of losing Jacob the way she had lost Jon and Arjan.

"It doesn't seem fair. I've tried," she blurted out one evening. "It's not that I don't want to change. It's just that people don't see I've changed! They won't let me see Jacob because they don't see me changing. Changing is hard, and it's slow! Why don't they see that I am trying? Why don't they see the progress I've made? Why doesn't anyone notice?"

Oksana's outburst had become typical, for now she often acted out her anger in words rather than fists. Her outbursts were often fierce. This time had been no exception and everyone sat quietly waiting for her fury to subside. But tonight, Sy would disregard this common practice and turn the tables, "Oksana, you've been talking about your-self for three months. We all know you've been through a lot. And we pray for you. But complaining about it over and over again does no good. You must understand, it's not about you, Oksana! It's about the sending of God. God loves the world, and he sent his Son here to make us and the world a better place. He wants all of us to participate in his mission. It's time you stopped thinking about how hard life is for Oksana and started participating in God's mission!"

This affront was too much for Oksana, and she flung herself weep-ing into Francine's arms. As she buried her head in embarrassment, despair, and desperation, she heard Francine softly say, "He is right, Oksana."

That night had been another waypoint for Oksana. Perhaps not as mysterious as July 4 at Plymouth Church of the Pilgrims, nor as momentous as her flight from the twin towers, or even as moving as Martin's conversion story at Indian Point. But something changed this day. Something changed in Oksana's purpose, in her reason for living, in her future.

At Sue's suggestion, Oksana began volunteering at a small shelter in Queens. A haven for those suffering from domestic violence, the women and men that came to the shelter began to affect Oksana. These were her kin. These were fellow travelers that had been on the route from being abused to abusing. They knew her. And she knew their jour-ney. She soon discovered the wisdom in Sue's suggestion, for these were travelers for whom she could serve as a guide.

ARJAN'S VOICE

Over the next year, Oksana became a leader of the shelter's Mon-day morning volunteers. In much the same way she had led the day school, she found fulfillment in helping others. But the shelter was dif-ferent than the day school. At the day school, she had been tempted to strike unruly children. Here at the shelter, she was solving the problem behind her violence.

At the same time, she began a certification course at an online university to counsel those suffering from intimate partner violence. There was even talk of Oksana being hired as the day manager of the shelter. The prospect of having her own apartment and some independence enthralled her. Francine had taken a new job as a manager of a small luggage store in the West Village, and Oksana longed to give her back her privacy.

One Saturday afternoon, the two were headed uptown to inspect an apartment when Francine's phone rang. It was the only phone between the two, and the caller asked for Oksana.

"Can we meet, Oksana? I did it. I told them everything. I'm sorry." Oksana knew Arjan's deep voice, and bidding Francine goodbye, she headed to the Flatiron District where Arjan worked.

Arjan looked shaken, sitting alone in a booth at the back of the coffee shop. Oksana thought he had been crying, though his long black eyelashes and deep-set eyes often made it hard for her to tell. "I've ruined you. I told everything. I'm so evil," were the first words he spoke after a long pause. "Will you forgive me?"

Something inside of Oksana wanted to return to her old way with Arjan. Something made her want to rise up and lash out, punishing him. But to her surprise, the anger rose and then disappeared. Somewhere in the stories she had heard about God's love and Jesus' forgiveness, a spark had been lit. But the spark did not grow into a fiery outburst. Instead, it grew into compassion.

Oksana looked at Arjan for what seemed like the first time. He was smaller and more vulnerable than she remembered. Since the day they woke up in bed together after her accident, he had been her confidant and counselor. But after many years of ignoring his needs, she found herself ready to console him. "I'm here, Arjan. I forgive you. Will you forgive me?" she said in a quiet, more calming tone than she was accustomed to using. And in some ways, her tone reminded her of the deep reassuring voice of Arjan.

HOW TO NAVIGATE WAYPOINT 3

3·A GET INVOLVED

President John F. Kennedy once said, "Leadership and learning are indispensable to each other."[21] At Waypoint 3, the traveler begins to understand that there can be no moving forward until one starts to serve others on God's behalf. But oftentimes, the traveler has no experience with this. Therefore, the journey here often involves volunteering, as Oksana did at the shelter in Queens. And it sometimes means volunteering even before a traveler thinks he or she is ready. Here are some things to keep in mind about volunteering.

3

INNER-LIFE GROWTH
Growth in understanding, serving of others, and participating in the mission of God to take his good news of love and forgiveness to others.

EXPECT FAILURES. Volunteers must roll up their sleeves and engage in actual ministry. Jesus sent out the twelve disciples along with thirty-six teams of two.[22] He did this even though he knew they were not ready for everything they would encounter. Jesus is all knowing, and he knew his disciples would flounder.[23] But Jesus chose not to prevent this. Because Jesus sometimes lets us flounder and fail, he ensures that lessons learned will not be forgotten. Therefore, don't fear failure; for even when we make mistakes, we can learn from them. No matter what the failures may be, God promises to never leave or forsake us.

BECOME AN APPRENTICE. Jesus did not leave his disciples without advice or follow-up. Jesus encouraged them to live with him,[24] travel with him,[25] watch him as he ministered,[26] report back to him,[27] and be accountable to him.[28] As a new volunteer, you need an extended time to learn. Find someone who will travel with you and teach you how to minister to others.

◆3-8◆ GET AN EDUCATION

Sometimes volunteers can get formal training, like through an online university, as Oksana did. And at other times, the volunteer can learn through training programs hosted by government, charity, or community organizations. But training involves three factors.

FACTOR 1: PREPARE FOR FAILURE. As noted above, the volunteer must expect challenges and difficulties, and prepare to meet them with prayer, fasting, meditation, and persistence. As the disciples learned, God may use failure as a teaching moment to drive home a lesson.[29]

FACTOR 2: PREPARE FOR MISTREATMENT. Ministering for a living God involves what Jesus described as the spiritual struggle between good and evil.[30] Thus, maltreatment, harassment, and even bullying are not absent in ministry, but expected. A traveler must be prepared for these challenges through prayer, fasting, and meditation.

FACTOR 3: PREPARE BIBLICALLY. To be effective, a leader must grow in scriptural knowledge along with practical knowledge. Keep grounded in the stories of God's men and women who have served others on his behalf.

QUESTIONS FOR REFLECTION

1. Do you have a small group where you regularly receive encouragement, fellowship, and accountability? What are the benefits of such a fellowship?
2. What is your story of mentoring? Are there things you learned? How would you do things differently in the future?

EMERGENCE

So remember, every picture tells a story, don't it.

—Rod Stewart and Ron Wood[1]

MINISTRY
EMERGENCE **2**

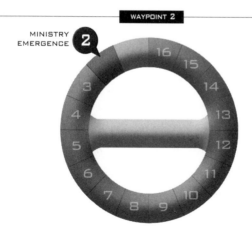

BY THE SUTLEJ RIVER

The water tickled her toes, and though this was the most solemn part of the ceremony, Oksana began to laugh. Arjan glanced sternly, but his glare from beneath a veil of flowers only made her giggle more. Arjan conjured an even more forbidding look, only to fail miserably as both he and Oksana broke into hearty laughter. Immediately, the singing of the hymns began to trail off, and there were awkward and disapproving glances from various attendees and officials. But this was Oksana's wedding, and she didn't care. The laughter and merriment symbolized her and Arjan's journey.

The river bank seemed the ideal place for a ceremony between two people who loved this country. And where better to be married in the land of five rivers, in Punjab, India, than on the banks of the Sutlej River? So much had happened in the last eighteen months. And as the ceremony was concluded with traditional hymns, the lyrical cadence of the songs led Oksana back to her memories of the long, strange journey that had led her here.

KUMARI

Kumari was unlike any other girl Oksana had helped at the shelter in New York. She was strong willed, outgoing, and fearless. Though Kumari was not her real name, she claimed it on her visa, for it was the Sanskrit word for lioness. But despite her boldness, Kumari always remained fully covered from head to foot. Only her olive-colored face would emerge from her deep blue clothing.

One winter day, while Oksana helped her out of a heavy overcoat, Kumari's left arm was exposed. "Kumari, what happened to you?" Oksana blurted out in reaction to Kumari's horribly burned arm. Kumari never replied, but soon Oksana learned that in her homeland, Kumari had been the victim of bride-burning.

Oksana came to learn that bride-burning is an illegal ritual, still practiced in some areas of India and Pakistan. A form of domestic violence, it occurs when a groom's family disapproves of a bride or when the bride's family provides too small of a dowry. In retaliation, the bride may be doused with a flammable liquid and set alight, leading to death.

"How could such a strong person like Kumari allow this to happen?" Oksana asked Francine during one of their weekly meetings. Oksana was at a loss for an answer until one of her visits with Father Henry.

"Oksana, a person may be bold and outgoing, but that does not mean she cannot be abused," responded Father Henry to Oksana's account. "You told me Kumari came to the shelter because of an abusive boyfriend here in America. Abuse knows no boundaries, no religion, no one personality type. It can happen to anyone, anywhere. And any abuse that leads to murder, such as bride-burning, is the most sinister."

REAL RELIGION

The words of Father Henry lingered in Oksana's mind. It was while pondering this that an old friend and colleague from Trinity, Stuart, reentered her life. Though still employed as the chaplain of Trinity Church, Stuart had been hired by the shelter to administer a survey to shelter workers. Oksana knew it had something to do with promotions, but more than this, she looked forward to becoming reacquainted with her old friend.

Stuart brought a survey he had used with the staff at Trinity. It looked for leadership traits that people might possess.[2] Stuart said it was based upon a study of the New Testament Scriptures. "These twenty-five traits are described in the Scriptures as 'gifts of the Holy Spirit,'" he explained. "That's because each person is given something to do to serve others and to show who God is." Stuart read, "God's various gifts are handed out everywhere; but they all originate in God's

Spirit. God's various ministries are carried out everywhere; but they all originate in God's Spirit. God's various expressions of power are in action everywhere; but God himself is behind it all. Each person is given something to do that shows who God is: Everyone gets in on it, everyone benefits. All kinds of things are handed out by the Spirit, and to all kinds of people! The variety is wonderful."[3]

Though Oksana found the terminology difficult to understand, the results made sense. "You have these gifts Oksana," Stuart concluded after tabulating the questionnaire. "You have the gifts of encouragement, hospitality, mercy, helps, and missionary."

It was this last term that bewildered her the most. She had always pictured missionaries as well-meaning do-gooders who lived in foreign cultures to manipulate and sway unsuspecting citizens. The idea that she might have a missionary gift was distasteful. "Why missionary?" she asked.

"Well Oksana, that's a person who participates in God's mission. His mission is to tell the world that he loves them, wants to help them, wants them to serve others, and wants them to live with him eternally," Stuart replied. "God has a mission, called the *missio Dei*. That just means the sending of God. God sends people to share this good news by serving others and telling them about his mission. When people carry out this mission in a culture that is not their own, they are called missionaries. They share God's good news by explaining who he is, but also by digging wells, giving medical attention, teaching in schools, righting wrongs, and standing up for the defenseless. The Bible says that 'Real religion, the kind that passes muster before God the Father, is this: Reach out to the homeless and loveless in their plight, and guard against corruption from the godless world.'"[4]

It was the words *reach out to the homeless and loveless in their plight,* that hit Oksana the deepest. And it was these words that led Oksana to turn down the opportunity to be the next director of the shelter in Queens. Instead, Oksana had traveled to the homeland of

Kumari, to work with a missionary agency in the Punjab region of India. And Arjan had followed. It was in those beautiful valleys that Oksana had grown to love the people of the Sutlej River region. And she had grown in her love for Arjan, as together they had grown in love for their Creator, the source of all love. Soulmates—theirs had become a deeply spiritual love.

Arjan reveled in his Sikh homeland. Yet Oksana had been drawn here not because of Arjan's love for these fertile valleys, nor Kumari's victimization here, but because she now understood what a missionary gift meant. She had developed from somewhere, exactly how or where she was not sure, an insatiable desire to help young girls who suffered from domestic violence, and specifically those threatened with dowry death and bride-burning.

Though outlawed for decades, dozens of women each year still died from such abuse in the small villages of the Punjab region. Stuart had located an Anglican missionary agency that worked to stop bride-burning. Oksana had been too determined to go to even invite Arjan. But he followed her.

HOW TO NAVIGATE WAYPOINT 2

Waypoint 2 is a locale where a traveler's God-given abilities begin to emerge.[5] The traveler often experiments with a variety of ministries, but also must be careful not to focus too narrowly. Usually a traveler has a mixture of gifts, as did Oksana.

> **MINISTRY EMERGENCE**
> Ministry increasingly becomes a focus of the traveler's life. Volunteering leads to experimentation with various ministries, and travelers discover their God-given gifts.

Traits and abilities can become supernaturally empowered by the Holy Spirit.[6] When they do, the Scriptures call them gifts of the Holy Spirit. According to the Scriptures, these gifts are given to all Christians. Here is what Oksana wrote down in her waypoint journal, underlining words that were important to her.

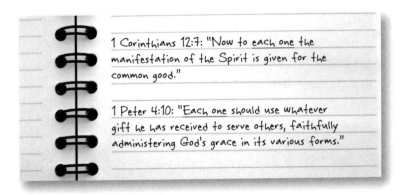

1 Corinthians 12:7: "Now to each one the manifestation of the Spirit is given for the common good."

1 Peter 4:10: "Each one should use whatever gift he has received to serve others, faithfully administering God's grace in its various forms."

2-A DISCOVER THE VARIETY OF SPIRITUAL GIFTS

Discovering your gifts begins with a study of the many spiritual gifts listed in the Scriptures. Here is a list with corresponding Scriptures.[7] You may want to look up some of the passages in your Bible.

Gift	Explanation	Scripture
Administration	Effective planning and organization	Acts 6:1–7; 1 Corinthians 2:28
Discernment	Distinguishing between error and truth	Acts 5:1–11; 1 Corinthians 12:10
Encouragement	Ability to comfort, console, encourage, and counsel	Romans 12:8; 1 Timothy 4:13; Hebrews 10:25
Evangelism	Building relationships that help travelers move toward a personal relationship with Christ	Luke 19:1–10; 2 Timothy 4:5
Faith	Discerning with extraordinary confidence the will and purposes of God	Acts 11:22–24; Romans 4:18–21; 1 Corinthians 12:9; Hebrews 11
Giving	Cheerfully giving of resources without remorse	Mark 12:41–44; Romans 12:8; 2 Corinthians 8:1–7; 9:2–8
Hospitality	Creating comfort and assistance for those in need[8]	Acts 16:14–15; Romans 12:9–13; 16:23; Hebrews 13:1–2; 1 Peter 4:9
Intercession	Passionate, extended, and effective prayer	Colossians 1:9–12; 4:12–13; 1 Timothy 2:1–2; James 5:14–16
Knowledge[9]	Discovering, analyzing, and clarifying information and ideas which are pertinent to the well-being of a Christian community	Acts 5:1–11; 1 Corinthians 2:14; 12:8; Colossians 2:2–3

Gift	Explanation	Scripture
Leadership	Casting vision, setting goals, and motivating others to cooperatively accomplish God's purposes	Luke 9:51; Romans 12:8; Hebrews 13:17
Mercy	Feeling authentic empathy and compassion accompanied by action that reflects Christ's love and alleviates suffering	Matthew 25:34–36; Luke 10:30–37; Romans 12:8
Prophecy[10]	Providing guidance by explaining and proclaiming God's truth	Acts 21:9–11; Romans 12:6; 1 Corinthians 12:10, 28; Ephesians 4:11–14
Helps	Investing time and talents in others to increase their effectiveness	Acts 9:36; Romans 16:1–2; 1 Corinthians 12:28
Service[11]	A tactical gift that identifies steps and processes in tasks	Acts 6:1–7; Romans 12:7; 2 Timothy 1:16–18
Pastor	Long-term personal responsibility for the welfare of spiritual travelers	John 10:1–18; Ephesians 4:1–14; 1 Timothy 3:1–7; 1 Peter 5:1–3
Teaching	Communicating relevant information that results in learning	Acts 18:24–28; 20:20–21; Romans 12:7; 1 Corinthians 12:28; Ephesians 4:11–14
Wisdom[12]	Having insight into how to apply knowledge	Acts 6:3, 10; 1 Corinthians 2:1–13; 12:8; James 1:5–6; 2 Peter 3:15–16
Missionary	Using spiritual gifts effectively in a culture they did not grow up in church	Acts 8:4; 13:2–3; 22:21; Romans 10:15; 1 Corinthians 9:19–21
Miracles	Performing compelling acts that are perceived by observers to have altered the ordinary course of nature	Acts 9:36–42; 19:11–20; 20:7–12; Romans 15:18–19; 1 Corinthians 12:10, 28; 2 Corinthians 12:12
Healing	Serving as human intermediaries through whom it pleases God to restore health	Acts 3:1–10; 5:12–16; 9:32–35; 28:7–10; 1 Corinthians 12:9, 28
Tongues[13]	This can mean: (a) to speak to God in a language a traveler has never learned; (b) to receive and communicate an immediate message of God to his people;[14] or (c) an ability to speak a foreign language and convey concepts across cultures	Acts 2:1–13; 10:44–46; 19:1–7; 1 Corinthians 12:10, 28; 14:13–19
Interpretation	Making known a message of one who speaks in tongues,[15] or "those who help build bridges across cultural, generational and language divides"[16]	1 Corinthians 12:10, 30; 14:13, 26–28
Voluntary Poverty	Renouncing material comfort and luxury to assist others	Acts 2:44–45; 4:34–37; 1 Corinthians 13:1–3; 2 Corinthians 6:10; 8:9
Celibacy	Remaining single with joy and not suffering undue sexual temptation	Matthew 19:10–12; 1 Corinthians 7:7–8

Gift	Explanation	Scripture
Martyrdom[17]	Ability to undergo suffering for the faith even to death, while displaying an attitude that brings glory to God	1 Corinthians 13:3
A gift that is not mentioned directly in the New Testament gift lists, but which is seen at other junctures in the Scriptures and church history.		
Artist[18]	The ability to communicate God's message via artistic mediums	1 Chronicles 5; Psalm 33:3; 42:8; 74:21; 149:1; 150; Ephesians 5:19; Colossians 3:16

2-B DISCOVER YOUR GIFTS BY FINDING A NEED AND MEETING IT

The next step is to look for a need that you can fill. The Scriptures say that the purpose of spiritual gifts is "the common good" and to "serve others." Oksana wrote in her waypoint journal (underlines are Oksana's).

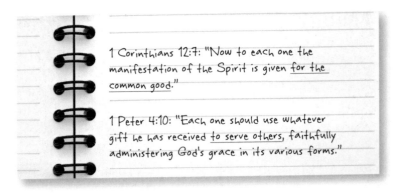

1 Corinthians 12:7: "Now to each one the manifestation of the Spirit is given for the common good."

1 Peter 4:10: "Each one should use whatever gift he has received to serve others, faithfully administering God's grace in its various forms."

2-C TEST YOUR GIFTS

One pastor said, "You discover a spiritual gift just like you discovered your natural talents." That means you try them out.[19] There are certainly some gifts that do not lend themselves to experimentation, such as the gift of martyrdom. But for most gifts, volunteering and testing them is a way to discover your God-given abilities. Oksana tested her gifts at the shelter at Queens, and she discovered she was effective when she used her gifts of encouragement, hospitality, mercy, and helps. And she received confirmation of her missionary gift when she began ministering effectively in a dissimilar culture.

◈ 2-D EXPECT CONFIRMATION

God gives good gifts to his children.[20] While exercising gifted-ness, a traveler should sense an inner confirmation. This has been called the "eureka" factor because a traveler will feel that "this, really, is what I had rather do for God than anything else in the world."[21]

The faith community should give confirmation too. When a traveler exercises God-given gifting, one that has been given "for the common good" and "to serve others," then the community of faith will recognize this.[22]

Oksana received confirmation both from her coworkers at the shelter and the leaders of the missionary agency that sent her to India. She now felt more alive and valued than at any time in her life. And despite her hardships and losses, Oksana began to feel at ease and rest.

QUESTIONS FOR REFLECTION

1. Look at the chart of gifts in this chapter (pages 108–110). Which gifts do you think you possess?

2. Have you experienced confirmation? Write how you have experienced confirmation in your waypoint journal.

IMPACT

Seek out that particular mental attribute which makes you feel most deeply and vitally alive, along with which comes the inner voice which says, "This is the real me," and when you have found that attitude, follow it.

—William James

IMPACT
EMERGENCE

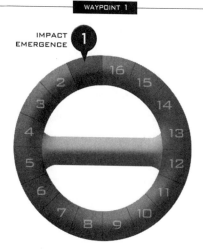

NEWS

Oksana was awoken by flashes of light outside her curtains. She had not heard thunder, and the flashes seemed too rapid to be a thunderstorm. Drawing herself from her bed, she looked outside to see Arjan facing a crowd of reporters. Even from this distance she could tell Arjan was getting frustrated. Her heart sank as she saw the expression on his face as he returned to the house.

"They are from as far away as Mumbai," he grumbled to her. "They won't take 'no comment' as an answer. They want to know about the lawsuit."

"Why would they even care?" came Oksana's reply. "That was over five years ago. That was settled out of court. They agreed not to say anything bad about me again."

"I know," replied Arjan. "But now that you are the missions director for Punjab and Uttarakhand, you are well-known here in New Delhi. They go fishing for things to write about such people. Besides, we still don't know who has been sending those e-mails to the newspapers." Pausing, and returning to the calm demeanor to which Oksana was accustomed, Arjan said thoughtfully, "Can't they just see the evidence of your life since then? You've never been accused of that again. People need to judge you on who you are, not what people said in an old lawsuit. A lawsuit they settled without an admission of guilt."

Eleven months had gone by since the wedding, and Oksana and Arjan had settled into a home in New Delhi. And though the lawsuit had been settled out of court without an admission of guilt, the Internet accusations dogged her, even to India. Someone had begun sending e-mails to the mission's supporters with a newspaper article about the old lawsuit, trying to make it sound as if it was recent. Oksana and Arjan's lawyer told them this was libel and criminal activity, and they should track down the perpetrators through their e-mails and countersue for millions. But the Indian authorities did not have the latest technology, so they waited for the next round of slander, prepared to follow any new trails to the guilty party.

In the meantime, Oksana and Arjan tried to keep the mission work going while ignoring the libelous e-mails. Oksana was now in charge of the mission's work in two Indian regions, and more than any other time in her life, she was enjoying her work. She delighted in organizing the dozens of missionary workers in Punjab and Uttarakhand. She linked her passion for the poor with an ability to expand the mission's work among the suffering. As a result, the missionary agency had tripled the number of people it was helping. And there had been talk about Oksana serving on a United Nations task force on bride burning. This would require her to travel back to New York City once a year. Oksana still missed its urban canyons and bustle. Occasional e-mails from Francine in New York reminded Oksana how far she had come. But they also brought back painful memories of when she first met Francine, and when Oksana still saw Jacob.

That talk came to fruition one humid, October morning three weeks later when Oksana received two unexpected visitors. The first was a representative of the missionary agency. "We want you to serve," were the words that struck Oksana. He had come to New Delhi to ask her to serve on a United Nations task force on bride burning. Though the topic was serious, Oksana was elated. She could now visit New York again. She could do some good by making the United Nations aware that thousands of young girls still die because of bride burning. And she could see Francine.

CATLIKE

A second visitor appeared about 7 p.m. that evening. Arjan answered the door, still wary of being waylaid by journalists. But the voice Oksana heard had a familiar ring. Running to the door, she cried half in disbelief and half in fear when she realized who it was: "Jon!"

Jon had been traveling through Southern Asia. He had lost his tour business during the recent recession—when sightseeing in the Outback dried up. Since then he had been traveling in search of new, less modernized countries where he could launch a new tour business. Jon's wife and Jacob had remained in Australia, while he began to work with potential business partners in Kenya. It was on his return from Mombasa that he arrived unannounced at Oksana's home in New Delhi.

It was almost thirty tense minutes before the reason for Jon's visit came into focus. "I know you have been having a time of it, Oksana," said Jon. "That's not right, how the reporters hound you. Not right. And I'm not one to see anyone wronged for something they said you did so long ago. But I've got to think of Jacob. I need to take care of him, and this job in Tsavo National Park in Kenja would help. I would be the private outfitter for the whole park. But the government is corrupt in Mombasa. I have to pay bribes. I don't have it, Oksana. But you could get it."

"How much money do you need," came Oksana's hesitant reply.

"Maybe ten thousand U.S. dollars. Maybe a little more," Jon said.

"Where am I going to find that kind of money, Jon? Our agency gives money to the poor. This conversation is over!" Oksana rose to show Jon the door.

"It's not over, Oksana," replied Jon in his exaggerated Outback drawl that she had heard so many times. This was the voice Jon used when he was about to show some naïve tourist an Outback spectacle. "I'm ready to tell 'em you hit me! Jacob, too. Think about it, Oksana. The media will never leave you alone once they hear this. That'll fix it so you'll never see Jacob again. But all it would take is a little money from your agency. You could pinch the money from here and there. Nobody would know. Isn't Jacob worth it?"

Suddenly, from the corner of the room burst what at first Oksana thought was a bush leopard. Never had she seen Arjan so aggressive and upset. He leapt upon Jon with a ferocity born of years of bottled-up anger and disdain. The chair broke beneath Jon, as he, too, had never anticipated anything so ferocious from Arjan. Within moments, Jon had fled. The sight of all two hundred and fifty pounds of Arjan descending upon him had driven the fortune-hunter from their home.

And in the corner of their disheveled room Oksana and Arjan wept.

How to Navigate Waypoint 1

Waypoint 1 is called "influence convergence" because it is a place where a traveler is utilizing his or her gift-mix so well that commendation results. Oksana had not only enjoyed her work in the upper regions of India,

1

> **IMPACT EMERGENCE**
> Ministry is supernaturally effective and widely recognized. Ministry and influence are maximized.

but she had found a job that matched her gifts and abilities as well. She was the happiest she had ever known. The people she served in the fields of Punjab and in the concrete canyons of New York City noticed too.

But Waypoint 1 is not a place that all travelers will reach. Some travel for years and never reach this place where ministry is maximized. But it is still a destination for which all humans long. It seemed to Oksana that God placed in her heart a knowledge that she could do something significant to meet the needs of others. It was not fame but having an effect that drove her. She wrote in her waypoint journal:

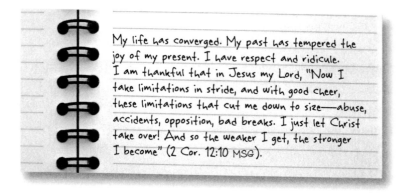

My life has converged. My past has tempered the joy of my present. I have respect and ridicule. I am thankful that in Jesus my Lord, "Now I take limitations in stride, and with good cheer, these limitations that cut me down to size—abuse, accidents, opposition, bad breaks. I just let Christ take over! And so the weaker I get, the stronger I become" (2 Cor. 12:10 MSG).

Signs of Travelers at Waypoint 1

1-A Regular People Are Leaders Too

Leaders at this waypoint often become increasingly aware that they are normal, with all the faults, idiosyncrasies, and failures that come with being human. As travelers negotiate this waypoint, they become increasingly honest about their shortcomings.

For example, at the height of the controversy over Rick Warren's participation at the inauguration of President Barak Obama, Warren was interviewed by NBC's Ann Curry. During their dialogue about whether homosexuality is determined by biology or experience, Warren replied, "Well, just because it seems natural doesn't mean it's best for you or society. I'm naturally inclined to have sex with every beautiful woman I see. But that doesn't mean it's the right thing to do . . . I think that's part of maturity. I think it's part of delayed gratification. I think it's part of character."[1] The interviewer was noticeably taken aback by Warren's response, but such candor is often a hallmark of those at Waypoint 1.

1-B They Lead the Kind of Ministry They Would Want to Join

Emerging leaders at Waypoint 1 see ministry as natural, enjoyable, and influential. They feel ministry is not something they are forced to do but something they are fortunate to do. They take pleasure in ministry because they are doing what they enjoy. And their sense of enjoyment inspires others to join them. Too often, travelers think they must copy another successful leader. This ignores the fact that God created an amazing array of different personalities, experiences, and environments. The Waypoint 1 traveler will resist a prefabricated approach to ministry and opt for an indigenous and authentic route to leadership that is comprised of six signposts.[2]

EMERGING LEADERS DISCOVER THEIR STRATEGIC, TACTICAL, OR OPERATIONAL STYLES. Leaders are usually strategic, tactical, or operational leaders.[3] Let's look briefly at each.

- Strategic leaders are big-picture people. They often see the future better than the present. They are motivated by vision and tend to be the senior leaders of churches, missionary agencies, and businesses. They tend to not understand or appreciate the steps that are required to get a job done. Thus, they like to leave the planning to tactical leaders. Oksana was not a strategic leader. She often did not understand the bigger picture, and without knowing it, she surrounded herself with big-picture people like Stuart, Father Henry, and eventually Arjan.
- Tactical leaders are skilled at organizing, planning, evaluation, and adjustment. Tactical leaders wait for the strategic leaders to set the direction with a vision, and then they go to work making step-by-step plans to bring about this vision. This was Oksana's gift. She skillfully organized the mission's work among dozens of missionaries in Punjab, Haryana, and Uttarakhand.
- Operational leaders lead small and skilled teams on critical assignments. They lead through the relationships they develop. Because they lead a small team, they "have an immediate, urgent, and vital task to perform. They may not see where their efforts fit into the bigger picture, but they are the masters of relational leadership."[4] This was also what Oksana liked doing. She enjoyed leading a small group in expanding the missionary work.

EMERGING LEADERS DISCOVER THE ABILITIES THEY ENJOY AND THOSE THEY DON'T. Leadership is based upon finding a job that the leader enjoys doing. But experiences, both good and bad, make leaders who they are. Leaders should expect to find some jobs that they don't enjoy and steer away from them.

EMERGING LEADERS WORK AS A TEAM. These leaders recognize they have certain skills, but they surround themselves with those who have skills that balance theirs. If leaders have little interest in creating budgets or financial planning, they should surround themselves with those who have such tactical skills. Emerging leadership is based upon teamwork and partnership.

EMERGING LEADERS ARE HONEST ABOUT WEAKNESSES. Emerging leaders recognize that all people, including leaders, are in the process of becoming more Christlike, and that they are not there yet. Therefore, emerging leaders exhibit the following behaviors:

- They are honest about personality weaknesses. Oftentimes a leader has been born with traits that make him or her insecure, overconfident, jealous, or angry. An emerging leader is honest, yet persistent in spiritual growth.
- They practice moral and ethical behavior. Good leaders have a high ethical standard to which they hold themselves.[5] But they do not wear their weakness on their sleeve as a badge of shame or pity. Instead, when they have a moral weakness, they acknowledge this to their spouse, pastors, or accountability parties. Through openness and honesty, emerging leaders create a team that helps them avoid moral and ethical failures.
- They rise above physical weaknesses. Scott Schmieding is a cancer survivor who pastors a growing church in Baton Rouge, Louisiana. Several years ago, Scott was diagnosed with throat cancer. Eventually losing his vocal cords, his book *Fighting Cancer with Faith* tells how faith helped him muster the strength to take on cancer. Though his vocal cords were damaged by the surgery and he was told his speech would be distracting and difficult to understand, Scott learned to speak again and returned to preaching. Though his speech has been affected, his listeners have become accustomed to his voice

and can understand him. Scott saw the loss of his voice as a setback to preaching ministry, but he also knew his fight would be a spiritual help to those experiencing the ups and downs of cancer—that it would feed people's faith to help them fight the disease. An emerging leader sees physical weakness as another obstruction on the journey that can be met and overcome with God's help.

EMERGING LEADERS TAKE THE ADVICE OF OTHERS SERIOUSLY. Good leaders do not shy away from what others say about them; they learn from it. They regularly ask others to give them input and advice.[6] Dr. Martin Luther King, Jr., in response to the Birmingham bombings, "Went to the privacy of a bedroom and summoned a diversity of opinions—from a Jew, a white person, an elderly person, a woman, and a close male confidant, more or less in that order. This moment symbolized . . . Dr. King's constant attention to getting a diverse input from everyone and building a broad coalition of supporters, regardless of race, religion, age, or gender."[7]

EMERGING LEADERS WELCOME COMPANIONS ON THEIR JOURNEY. Good leaders are often accompanied by the fellowship of fellow travelers who have willingly and cheerfully joined them on the journey. On her spiritual journey, Oksana enjoyed the advice and accompaniment of a variety of companions including Stuart, Father Henry, Louise, Martin, Francine, and Arjan.

QUESTIONS FOR REFLECTION

1. What does your ideal ministry look like? Describe this ministry in your waypoint journal.
2. Without being graphic or shocking, answer honestly: Are there shortcomings, weaknesses, and temptations that you would like friends or colleagues to help you overcome? Write these weaknesses and shortcomings in your waypoint journal.

CONVERGENCE

This is the true joy in life—being used for a purpose recognized
by yourself as a mighty one; the being thoroughly worn out
before you are thrown on the scrap heap.

—George Bernard Shaw[1]

WAYPOINT 0

END OF THE DAY

"Ouch! That's the third time," protested Oksana as she examined the needle pricks on her finger.

"You cannot rush sewing. If you don't slow down, you'll keep making mistakes, and we'll be here until dawn," came Arjan's unhurried reply.

This was Oksana's first Republic Day parade, and she was determined to wear her favorite sari despite its torn hem. She was so honored to be riding in a float representing Punjab. She knew this was India's largest national celebration, and she had been almost speechless when asked by the Punjab government to represent their state.

Out of the corner of her eye, Oksana saw Arjan's figure standing over her, arms crossed. She looked up to see that broad smile she so adored. He was just shaking his head.

"What?" She laughed, glancing back at her still-aching finger.

"Padma Vibhusha!" burst Arjan. He grasped both of her hands and clamped them to his breast. Never had Oksana expected this honor.

"First my father," continued Arjan. "And now you, Oksana."

THE TRUMPET'S BLAST

Oksana jerked from her shallow slumber. She didn't know how she could fall asleep so quickly, or at such a serious time. But she had.

The trumpet was signaling the entrance of the flag carriers, and Oksana was thankful their pageantry took all eyes away from her errant nap.

Within what seemed like only a few minutes the ceremony was over. Oksana had received the 2015 Padma Vibhusha Award, India's second-highest award, rarely given to non-citizens. The official had spoken graciously of her many years of work among the young women of the Punjab and Uttarakhand regions, then emphasizing her influential work at the United Nations. Her love for their people had endeared her to her adopted homeland.

She looked back at Arjan, seated several rows behind her. He still smiled broadly.

He could not look prouder. This was after all the same award his father had received in 1965 for military service. She thought how different he was from his father. His father had been a daring man of war, almost reckless. Arjan had inherited his father's ability to think through almost any hopeless situation. But Arjan was kinder, more cautious. She wondered how she could have survived life's journey without him. And she wondered why God would choose her for such blessings and honor. After all, she was just a child of the Midwest, born of Russian parents, and had made many mistakes. But God had used everything, even her mistakes, in ways she had never imagined.

As she pondered these things, the trumpet grew louder. It beautifully represented her acceptance speech, which she had titled simply, "Blow a Trumpet." It was only two paragraphs long. In fact, in her speech she would simply read from her waypoint journal, where she had scribbled down 1 Corinthians 1:26.

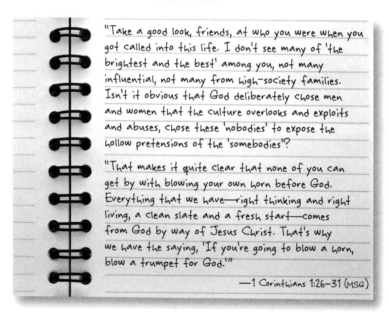

"Take a good look, friends, at who you were when you got called into this life. I don't see many of 'the brightest and the best' among you, not many influential, not many from high-society families. Isn't it obvious that God deliberately chose men and women that the culture overlooks and exploits and abuses, chose these 'nobodies' to expose the hollow pretensions of the 'somebodies'?

"That makes it quite clear that none of you can get by with blowing your own horn before God. Everything that we have—right thinking and right living, a clean slate and a fresh start—comes from God by way of Jesus Christ. That's why we have the saying, 'If you're going to blow a horn, blow a trumpet for God.'"

—1 Corinthians 1:26–31 (MSG)

But suddenly the stage floor turned to quicksand, and the clamoring, smiling crowd vanished into a thick blackness.

Oksana seemed to be entering a narrow and dark hallway. "Chicago?" she cried out—"Francine?" She seemed to have abruptly entered a room, where for some reason she was expecting to find Francine and her Latina friends. But instead, a bright light, as bright as the sun, greeted her.

And then, profound pain finally caught her, so excruciatingly that she could no longer see or hear.

She remembered no more.

LUDHIANA

The sign above the door made Oksana uneasy: "Palliative Care Clinic and Christian Medical College of Ludhiana, Punjab." She still did not know what *palliative* meant, but she knew this would likely be the doorway to the next part of her journey. The excruciating moment had proven to be an indication of what doctors seemed 95 percent certain must be a fatal outcome. There was no cure.

"We have everything ready. You will be comfortable and cared for. And we are excited to have such a distinguished person with us," explained the balding short man who escorted her.

From down the hallway, Oksana could see faces peering. Most were gaunt with deep set eyes. She marveled how beautiful the eyes of the Indian people were, even when so hollow.

As she walked down the corridor, residents struggled to touch her. One older woman kissed her on the cheek, and another gave her a small hand-sewn blanket. At the end of the hallway were two rooms. The one to the right housed a small table where an orderly sat smoking. Across the hallway was her small dim room with its neatly made bed.

Oksana fell onto the bed, exhausted from her walk down the hallway. And then once again, the room darkened and Oksana wondered why night should come so early.

But since those days in the Never-Never so long ago, darkness would not frighten her. In some regards, it was her friend. It was where she had encountered the stories of faith in Gulingi, where the wind had been her constant companion, where Jon had rescued her, where Stuart had guided her to safety, and where she had been changed in the sanctuary of Plymouth Church of the Pilgrims. For Oksana, darkness seemed a spiritual place, a place of redemption and a place of transformation.

When Oksana awoke, the man smoking the cigarette was there, ready to change her sheets. He began to speak without looking up. "You've been sleeping for three days. Thought you might never wake up. Here, you've gone and soaked these bed-sheets again." And with that he hurried from the room carrying a large bundle of cloth.

But Oksana was remembering, and it was so wonderful to remember. She thought back to her wedding day with Arjan. Not the wedding day on the Sutlej River, but her wedding day outside of Chicago, when she and Arjan were first married.

The eleven years had reappeared like a long-lost friend. She remembered her love and passion for Arjan—for his patient and kind ways. Joy spread more deeply into her soul than she had ever known. She at last knew why there could be no other.

And then Arjan entered her room. She smiled and started to cry out his name, but only the sound of a slight wind came from her lips. The doctor followed close behind him. Arjan looked deep into her eyes with his sad, but still familiar smile. She wanted to tell him that those missing eleven years had returned. She wanted to tell him she now remembered when she first fell in love with him. But a look in his eyes told her that he knew.

She struggled to raise her head. Arjan lifted it into his shoulder. There was that smell. The smell of Arjan. That was the most beautiful scent in all life.

But then the darkness returned.

TRAVELERS

Each time she awoke, Oksana found it harder to throw off the beckoning darkness of sleep. But once more she struggled to raise her head. She felt a warm hand place a small pillow behind her neck.

She opened her eyes carefully. She could see three figures standing at her bedside. The one in white must be the doctor, and Arjan's larger profile was unmistakable. The third was thinner, thinner than any person she had seen outside of this hospice.

"Jon!" she exclaimed in a voice that only she could hear.

He looked old and washed out—empty, almost devoid of frame. He had never been a big man like Arjan, but Jon was a bush guide and a decade or so ago he'd had an imposing physique.

"Jon is here to see you Oksana," came Arjan's voice at last. "He's got something to say." Arjan stepped back out of view.

The room fell silent—peacefully still for some time. She felt the darkness of sleep beckoning. Then Jon began, head bowed, quietly, "I never should have taken Jacob. He's always been more of you. And I never should have lied to keep you away." Jon's voice faltered, and he looked up into Oksana's eyes with a pleading desperation. "And I'm afraid. Can you pray?"

Oksana was finding it difficult to focus. All she could see was the outline of a broken, ill, little man. Yet his plea for prayer reminded her of the innocent young voice of Jacob. And though Jon had always stood between her and her son, his voice beckoned her.

Though her lips moved, no sound emerged. But Jon knew that Oksana was praying, as a mother and a spouse. She fought off the darkness several times as her lips moved silently. And once she mouthed her amen, sleep overtook her.

Memories and images from the past swirled in Oksana's head. These dreams seemed more vivid than any she had experienced. Aboriginal dancers were interspersed with falling buildings, coffees with Francine, the oak knoll of Indian Point, Sy and Jimmy's apartment, and a host of other vistas.

Finally, in the middle of this whirlwind, Arjan beckoned. He called out to her, and she realized she was still propped in bed. But Jon was now gone. In his place were two men. She could barely make out their clerical collars, but she knew immediately from his imposing stature that one was Stuart. The other, shorter figure she couldn't make out. She wondered if it could be Father Henry. "They want to pray for you Oksana," came Arjan's calm voice.

Stuart came close, and she felt his breath upon her face. He prayed long and passionately for Jesus to guide Oksana. She felt a sense of completion, for Stuart was relinquishing his role as her guide.

Then the priest approached. His hands were cold as he grasped hers. As he leaned forward, she felt a wetness on her cheek. "May I give you last rights?" came his soft request.

Oksana did not know if she acknowledged, but he began his prayer. In his gentle words, she felt a cycle of completion. Her life felt as if it had come full circle. For a moment, she felt like a young mother again, cuddling her child close to her breast.

Life had been good. And the road, worthwhile.

And then the priest concluded his prayer.

Oksana's eyes cleared for an instant. She looked deep and longingly into the priest's face. She looked as if to see one last glimpse into a life well-traveled.

And then, Oksana passed the final waypoint of this life. And on her smiling lips was a single, simple word.

"Jacob."

How to Navigate Waypoint O

CONVERGENCE

Here, a traveler's ministry has become widely influential over a period of time. Characterized by humility and grace, this has been described as a "ministry afterglow." It foreshadows a final convergence.

Because the converging leader is working from gifts and strengths and not from areas in which he or she is not gifted, ministry is maximized. Such effective ministry gains widespread attention, as did Oksana's when she joined the United Nations task force on bride burning and was awarded the Padma Vibhusha.

Leaders who reach convergence recognize that any honor they receive is undeserved and belongs to God. They realize that God has given them these opportunities. And they seek to honor God by telling others that this is God's work, as did Oksana in her acceptance speech.

Oksana's early errors in her journey continued to haunt her most of her life through media scrutiny and Jon's extortions. Yet, it always seemed remarkable to Oksana that God chose her and not someone who was flawless.

Many times, for reasons known only to God, deserving travelers may never reach ministry convergence. Yet all travelers on life's road will reach the final convergence.

Actions That Help Waypoint O Travelers

O-A Free to Empower Others

Converging leaders empower others. The world is underserved if only professional ministers do the serving. God intended for ordinary people to do the majority of his work. Jesus delegated his authority to ordinary disciples, sending them out to carry his ministry into needy communities. Here are some Scriptures Oksana first discovered at Sy and Jimmy's apartment. She wrote them down in her waypoint journal.

Delegating to the Twelve

"Jesus now called the Twelve and gave them authority and power to deal with all the demons and cure diseases. He commissioned them to preach the news of God's kingdom and heal the sick. He said, 'Don't load yourselves up with equipment. Keep it simple; you are the equipment. And no luxury inns—get a modest place and be content there until you leave. If you're not welcomed, leave town. Don't make a scene. Shrug your shoulders and move on.' Commissioned, they left. They traveled from town to town telling the latest news of God, the Message, and curing people everywhere they went."

—Luke 9:1-6 (MSG)

Delegating to All Followers

"God authorized and commanded me to commission you: Go out and train everyone you meet, far and near, in this way of life, marking them by baptism in the threefold name: Father, Son, and Holy Spirit. Then instruct them in the practice of all I have commanded you. I'll be with you as you do this, day after day after day, right up to the end of the age."

—Matthew 28:18-20 (MSG)

D-8 ▷ FREE TO GIVE YOUR BEST

CONVERGING LEADERS DISCOVER THE FOCUS OF THEIR GIFTS. Converging leadership is organic, rising from the unique gift-mix of the individual, coupled with God-given opportunities. Converging leaders "minister out of what they are."[2] After many years of difficult ministry, Oksana's ministry came into focus.

CONVERGING LEADERS STAY FOCUSED ON BIBLICAL PRINCIPLES BECAUSE THEY ARE "TRAINING US TO LIVE GOD'S WAY."[3] The leader keeps grounded in regular study of the Bible. Here is one of the many Bible passages Oksana wrote in her journal:

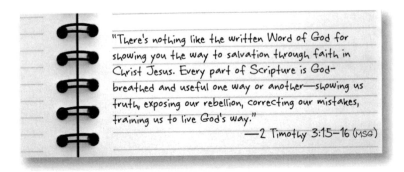

"There's nothing like the written Word of God for showing you the way to salvation through faith in Christ Jesus. Every part of Scripture is God-breathed and useful one way or another—showing us truth, exposing our rebellion, correcting our mistakes, training us to live God's way."
—2 Timothy 3:15–16 (MSG)

CONVERGING LEADERS ARE ORGANIC AND AUTHENTIC. Finally, converging leaders recognize that many experiences, failures, and undeserved opportunities have led them to where they are. They do not take credit themselves, for not only have they been blessed, but they have stumbled as well.

Oksana made many mistakes in her early years of ministry, even blamed for things she did not do. But these learning experiences, both deserved and unjustified, equipped her to be a better mentor to other missionaries. Oksana's journey, the good, the bad, and the groundless, shaped her life. After many years of blameless ministry, time had been Oksana's advocate and defender.

She could now experience the ultimate convergence, free from blame.

◇ D-C ◇ FREE FROM THIS WORLD

ALL TRAVELERS WILL LEAVE THIS WORLD. Ministry convergence foreshadows life's convergence. In Oksana's last minutes on her spiritual journey, she radiated the same love, forgiveness, and grace that grew out of her travels. And though fleeting, her traits and lessons from life would inspire thousands.

THE CONVERGING LEADER DOES NOT FEAR DEATH. Death is not an end, but a doorway into another realm. Here is the last passage that Oksana scribbled in her waypoint journal. Jacob would long after keep his mother's journal at his bedside and open it often to this passage.

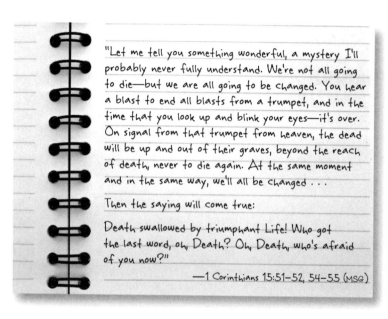

"Let me tell you something wonderful, a mystery I'll probably never fully understand. We're not all going to die—but we are all going to be changed. You hear a blast to end all blasts from a trumpet, and in the time that you look up and blink your eyes—it's over. On signal from that trumpet from heaven, the dead will be up and out of their graves, beyond the reach of death, never to die again. At the same moment and in the same way, we'll all be changed . . .

Then the saying will come true:

Death swallowed by triumphant Life! Who got the last word, oh, Death? Oh, Death, who's afraid of you now?"

—1 Corinthians 15:51–52, 54–55 (MSG)

QUESTIONS FOR PERSONAL REFLECTION

1. What lessons have you learned from your failures? Are they more or less helpful with your ministry to other leaders? (There is no right answer here.) Do you often want to avoid discussing lessons learned from failures because they are embarrassing? Is this good or bad? How will you help others avoid your leadership failures?

2. How do you view the ultimate convergence: death? Look at the last Bible passage Oksana wrote in her waypoint journal. Write a paragraph about your feelings on this.

AFTERWORD

Anyone who sets himself up as "religious" by talking a good game is
self-deceived. This kind of religion is hot air and only hot air. Real
religion, the kind that passes muster before God the Father, is this:
Reach out to the homeless and loveless in their plight, and
guard against corruption from the godless world.

—James[1]

As you have noticed, before the end of life's journey come many
opportunities to help others. And successfully traversing a waypoint gives
the traveler an opportunity to help others navigate that same waypoint.
That's what it's all about. That's why we are on this journey—to walk
with God, yes, but in doing so, to help others in their journeys too—even
to walk the way with them. It's the meaning of your journey—the
meaning of your life.

On one occasion toward the end of his ministry, Jesus was challenged
by religious skeptics with several difficult questions, to each of
which he gave a brilliant but often confounding response. So, they
finally challenged him with the big question—effectively, they
asked him to sum up everything about Christianity. What's the
most important thing? For the purposes of this book, what's the

outcome we're ultimately looking for in our journey through the waypoints?

Jesus' answer? "'Love the Lord your God with all your heart and with all your soul and with all your mind.' This is the first and greatest commandment. And the second is like it: 'Love your neighbor as yourself.' All the Law and the Prophets hang on these two commandments."[2]

Loving God makes sense. But Jesus insisted the second greatest commandment (to love those around you—those who are in your reach of influence) is very much like the first: loving God. You can't truly be a spiritually alive person who claims to love God if you won't love other people. If you cannot do the second, you're not doing the first.

That's what the waypoints are about—the journey toward loving God well. But then what Christians are also about is like that first objective: loving your neighbor enough to help him or her find the way too. Waypointing is all about finding our way together.

At another time, Jesus described himself as the only way to the Father—not just what he was teaching or facts or information, but Jesus personally is the way.[3] That's because with God, it is always personal, always about relationship. He ultimately wants us to be about loving him and loving other people.

When Jesus said he was the way, that was his point.[*]

Are You Converging? (Circle the answers that best describe your feelings.)		
	Unfocused Spiritual Gifts	**Focused Spiritual Gifts**
At the end of the day:	You feel tired and worn out.	You feel tired, but it is a good tired. You feel you have used the gifts you enjoy, and that you made a positive impact.
In your understanding of spiritual gifts:	You do not see clearly how your various spiritual gifts complement one another.	You see that your spiritual gifts form a complementary matrix where each one builds upon the other.

	Unfocused Spiritual Gifts	Focused Spiritual Gifts
Your coworkers and friends:	They rely upon you to get things done. You have to constantly take the initiative.	They complement you, having strengths where you have weaknesses. You form an inter-reliant team with other leaders.
Serving Jesus:	Is something that must be done, and you labor at doing it.	Is a joy and a blessing. You feel tired, but more so, inspired.
The needy and oppressed:	Their situation is the result of a fallen world. You despise the forces that have imprisoned them, and meeting their needs is laborious and painstaking.	They are made in the *imageo Dei*, God's image, and you love them and what Christ can do for them more than you despise the forces that put them there.
The church:	Is comprised of a petty alliance of dissenters, critics, and culturally captive advocates. Playing politics is necessary to lead them.	Is an errant yet beloved community for whom Christ died. As a fellowship of the cross, they help the leader and each other overcome the obstacles and detours of the journey.
In the future:	The pastor will labor in ministry until death or burnout (the former is preferred).	The pastor will journey through the trials and triumphs of ministry, and in the end mirror Shaw's description of Bunyan's Christian: "This is the true joy in life—being used for a purpose recognized by yourself as a mighty one."[4]

*For information and resources to help others find their own waypoints, visit: www.wesleyan.org/wph/waypoint.

WAYPOINTS

16	No awareness of a supreme being
15	Awareness of a supreme being, no knowledge of the good news
14	Initial awareness of the good news
13	Awareness of the fundamentals of the good news
12	Grasp of the implications of the good news
11	Positive attitude toward the good news
10	Personal problem recognition
9	Decision to act
8	Repentance and faith in Christ
7	**NEW BIRTH**
6	Post-decision evaluation
5	Incorporation into the body
4	Spiritual foundations (conceptual and behavioral growth)
3	Inner-life growth (deepening communion with God)
2	Ministry emergence (spiritual gifts emerge)
1	Impact emergence (life influences others)
0	Convergence (experience, gifts, and influence converge into a life of integrity and inspiration)

NOTES

INTRODUCTION

1. Esther de Waal, *Seeking God: The Way of St. Benedict* (Collegeville, Minn.: Liturgical Press, 2001), 69.

2. Lesslie Newbigin, *The Gospel in a Pluralistic Society* (Grand Rapids, Mich.: Eerdmans, 1989), 183.

3. Ed L. Miller, *Questions That Matter: An Invitation to Philosophy* (New York: McGraw-Hill, 1996), 334.

4. "The tremendous mystery" is a translation of Rudolf Otto's *mysterium tremendum* in Rudolf Otto, *The Idea of the Holy*, trans. John W. Harvey (New York: Oxford University Press, 1950), 12–13.

5. Miller, *Questions That Matter*, 334.

CHAPTER 1

1. Though much of the narrative in this book is fictional, this quote and others (where noted) are actual Aboriginal dialogue as recorded in Harvey Arden's *Dreamkeepers: A Spirit-Journey into Aboriginal Australia* (New York: HarperOne, 1995). Those who would like a fuller understanding of the Australian Aboriginal culture should read Arden's engaging book.

2. Barry A. Kosmin and Ariela Keysar, *The American Religious Identification Survey (ARIS) 2008* (Hartford, Conn.: Program on Public Values, 2009), 4.

3. Christopher Hitchens, *God Is Not Great: How Religion Poisons Everything* (New York: Twelve Hachette Book Group, 2007), 160.

4. Adapted from Abraham H. Maslow, *Motivation and Personality*, 2nd ed. (New York: Harper and Row, 1970), 300–394; and Abraham H. Maslow, *The Farther Reaches of Human Nature* (New York: Viking Press, 1971), 300.

5. Ibid.

6. Jesus quoted in Luke 12:48 NKJV.

7. Arden, *Dreamkeepers*.

8. Sensing "a story behind all stories" is not new, nor limited to Oksana. In the popular *Star Trek* series, Captain James T. Kirk observes, "most mythology has its basis in fact" as quoted in Ross Kraemer, William Cassidy, and Susan L Schwartz, *Religions of Star Trek* (New York: Basic Books, 2008), 15. This book offers an interesting overview of the *Star Trek* franchise and their take on religion and the existence of God. While the series takes dim views of religion, it does embrace the idea of a god behind the universe (such as, "The Apple," 1967; "Who Morns for Adonais?" 1968, "Who Watches the Watchers," 1989, and "Devil's Due," 1991). Thus, the *Star Trek* franchise by embracing god without religion may actually be stuck in an orbit around Waypoint 15.

9. C. S. "Jack" Lewis, *Surprised by Joy: The Shape of My Early Life* (New York: Harcourt, Brace and World, 1955). See also the critical analysis of Lewis's change in John Beversluis's *C. S. Lewis and the Search for Rational Religion* (New York: Prometheus Books, 2007).

10. C. S. Lewis felt there was a true story behind or "reflected" in the many myths he studied. He also thought that the imagination, such as encountered in fantasy writings, could also "reflect" this story behind the story, *Surprised by Joy*, 167ff. Therefore, it is not surprising that C. S. Lewis would (along with his mentor in writing, George McDonald, and colleague J. R. R. Tolkien) pen numerous fantasy books that reflected a supernatural story.

11. Lewis, *Surprised by Joy*, 175.

12. Matthew 25:35–40 MSG.

13. This section deals in brief form with what Thomas Aquinas called the "Five Ways" to prove God's existence. While an extended examination of these five ways is beyond the scope of this book, the traveler looking for a helpful overview should see William Lane Craig's "Five Reasons God Exists," in *God?: A Debate between a Christian and an Atheist*, the Point/Counterpoint series (Oxford: Oxford University Press, 2004), 28.

14. Psalm 19:1 MSG.

15. Scientists such as Stephen Hawking rightly declare that "almost everyone now believes the universe, and time itself, had a beginning at the Big Bang." Stephen Hawking and Robert Penrose, *The Nature of Time and Space* (Princeton, N.J.: Princeton University Press, 1996), 20.

16. Jastrow goes on to say, "For the scientist who has lived by his faith in the power of reason, the story ends like a bad dream. He has scaled the mountains of ignorance; he is about to conquer the highest peak; as he pulls himself over the final rock, he is greeted by a band of theologians who have been sitting there for centuries." Robert Jastrow, *God and the Astronomers* (New York: Warner Books, 1978), 115–116.

17. Kai Nielsen, *Reason and Practice* (New York: Harper & Row, 1971), 48.

18. John Boslough, *Stephen Hawking's Universe: An Introduction to the Most Remarkable Scientist* (New York: HarperCollins, 1989), 109.

19. This is St. Thomas Aquinas's "Fifth Way" of knowing that God exists. Though it is difficult reading, the traveler who wishes to know more about Aquinas's arguments for God's existence should see St. Thomas Aquinas, *Summa Theologiae*, Pt. 1, Qu. 2. 3, *Basic Writings of St. Thomas Aquinas*, ed. Anton C. Pegis (New York: Random House, 1945), I.

20. Steve Paulson, "The Believer," http://www.salon.com/books/int/2006/08/07/collins/index2.html. In addition, Francis Collins' arguments for the existence of God and the compatibility of science can be found in Francis Collins, *The Language of God: A Scientist Presents Evidence for Belief* (New York: Free Press, 2007), 57–84; and Francis Collins, *Coming to Peace with Science: Bridging the Worlds Between Faith and Biology* (Downers Grove, Ill.: InterVarsity Press, 2004).

21. Francis Collins quoted by David van Biema, "God vs. Science: Can Religion Stand Up to the Test?" *Time*, November 5, 2006, 52. For more on Francis Collins's change of mind see *There Is a God: How the World's Most Notorious Atheist Changed His Mind* by Anthony Flew (New York: Harper-One, 2008).

CHAPTER 2

1. Tim Cahill, *Road Fever* (New York: Vintage Books, 1992), vii.

2. C. S. Lewis, "Christian Apologetics," *God in the Dock* (Grand Rapids, Mich.: Eerdmans), 101.

3. John 14:1–3.

4. John 14:6.

5. John 14:1–3.

6. 1 Peter 1:3–4.

7. Those at Waypoint 13 are usually inquisitive, curious, perplexed, and frustrated by all things spiritual. They have been drawn to further investigate their initial experience with religion at Waypoint 14. Such curiosity and frustration should be expected and accommodated by fellow travelers.

8. Space in this book does not allow for all major religions to be investigated. Therefore, this book will only consider the religions that Oksana encountered on her route to spiritual discovery. I believe it is healthy to investigate different religions, as I have done. But it is also my firm conviction that in doing so, the one and true religious path will emerge.

9. It is my firm conviction, for I have seen this in my own spiritual journey, that if a spiritual traveler is exposed to many different religions that the true religion will be evident in contrast to the others.

10. If you cannot agree on a translation, write down the word or concept in your waypoint journal and ask a different religious person for clarification when the opportunity arises.

11. Because Oksana's story is a fictional narrative, this chart is not penned by her. However, this chart was adapted from the book on comparative religions by Fritz Ridenour, *So What's the Difference: A Look at 20 Worldviews, Faiths and Religions and How They Compare to Christianity* (Ventura, Calif.: Regal Books, 2001). In addition, this chart is not exhaustive. Rather, this is an example of what a traveler might create after an initial investigation into different religions.

12. Deuteronomy 6:4.

13. Matthew 28:19.

14. John 4:25–26.

15. John 3:16.

16. Surah 4:157.

17. John 14:6.

18. 1 Samuel 28:12–15.

Chapter 3

1. Susan Sontag, *Styles of Radical Will* (New York: Macmillan, 2002), 75.

2. A recent survey indicates that most of North Americans consider themselves to be religious but do not necessarily embrace a Christian belief; Barry A. Kosmin and Ariela Keysar, *The American Religious Identification Survey (ARIS) 2008* (Hartford, Conn.: Program on Public Values, 2009), i.

3. Eddie Gibbs and Ryan K. Bolger, *Creating Christian Community in Postmodern Cultures* (Grand Rapids, Mich.: Baker Academic, 2005).

4. Isaiah 45:21–22.

5. Romans 3:23.

6. 1 John 1:8.

7. 1 John 1:8–9.

8. 2 Timothy 3:15–16 MSG.

9. Romans 10:9.

10. 1 Corinthians 12:4, 6–8 MSG.

11. Romans 12; 1 Corinthians 12; and Ephesians 4, along with secondary lists in 1 Corinthians 7; 13–14; Ephesians 3; and 1 Peter 4, describe many of the "gifts of the [Holy] Spirit" that God uses to empower people for service and ministry. These descriptions are adapted from the United Methodist Church's *Explore Your Spiritual Gifts* (http://www.umc.org/site/c.lwL4KnN1LtH/b.1355371/k.9501/Spiritual_Gifts.htm, 2009); Jack W. MacGorman's *The Gifts of the Spirit* (Nashville: Broadman Press, 1974); Kenneth C. Kinghorn's *Gifts of the Spirit* (Nashville: Abingdon Press, 1976); and C. Peter Wagner's *Your Spiritual Gifts Can Help Your Church Grow: How to Find Your Gifts and Use*

Them to Bless Others (Ventura, Calif.: Regal Books, 1994). For an extended discussion of these gifts see Waypoint 2.

12. This gift list has been abbreviated to those Oksana observed in Francine and wrote in her waypoint journal. Those gifts not listed by Oksana, but mentioned in the Bible include the following:

- Leadership: To cast vision, set goals, and motivate to cooperatively accomplish God's purposes (Luke 9:51; Rom. 12:8; Heb. 13:17).
- Administration: Effective planning and organization (Acts 6:1–7; 1 Cor. 2:28).
- Discernment: Distinguishing between error and truth (Acts 5:1–11; 1 Cor. 12:10).
- Knowledge: To discover, accumulate, analyze, and clarify information and ideas which are pertinent to the well being of a Christian community (Acts 5:1–11; 1 Cor. 2:14; 12:8; Col. 2:2–3).
- Prophecy: Providing guidance to others by explaining and proclaiming God's truth (Acts 21:9–11; Rom. 12:6; 1 Cor. 12:10, 28; Eph. 4:11–14).
- Service: A tactical gift that identifies steps and processes in tasks that results in ministry to others (Acts 6:1–7; Rom. 12:7; 2 Tim. 1:16–18).
- Pastor: Long-term personal responsibility for the welfare of spiritual travelers (John 10:1–18; Eph. 4:1–14; 1 Tim. 3:1–7; 1 Pet. 5:1–3).
- Wisdom: To have insight into how to apply knowledge (Acts 6:3, 10; 1 Cor. 2:1–13; 12:8; James 1:5–6; 2 Pet. 3:15–16).
- Missionary: Using spiritual gifts effectively in a non-indigenous culture (Acts 8:4; 13:2–3; 22:21; Rom. 10:15; 1 Cor. 9:19–21).
- Miracles: To perform compelling acts that are perceived by observers to have altered the ordinary course of nature (Acts 9:36–42; 19:11–20; 20:7–12; Rom. 15:18–19; 1 Cor. 12:10, 28; 2 Cor. 12:12).
- Healing: To serve as human intermediaries through whom it pleases God to restore health (Acts 3:1–10; 5:12–16; 9:32–35; 28:7–10; 1 Cor. 12:9, 28).
- Tongues: There are various explanations of this gift. For instance, it can be to (a) speak to God in a language they have never learned, and/or (b) to receive and communicate an immediate message of God to his people. Another option is that this can mean an ability to speak a foreign language and convey concepts across cultures (Acts 2:1–13; 10:44–46; 19:1–7; 1 Cor. 12:10, 28; 14:13–19).
- Interpretation: To make known a message of one who speaks in tongues. Or it can mean those who help build bridges across cultural, generational and language divides (1 Cor. 12:10, 30; 14:13, 26–28).
- Voluntary Poverty: To renounce material comfort and luxury to assist others (Acts 2:44–45; 4:34–37; 1 Cor. 13:1–3; 2 Cor. 6:10; 8:9).
- Celibacy: To remain single with joy and not suffer undue sexual temptation (Matt. 19:10–12; 1 Cor. 7:7–8).

- Martyrdom: Ability to undergo suffering for the faith even to death, while displaying a victorious attitude that brings glory to God (1 Cor. 13:3).

13. The gift of encouragement: Romans 12:8; 1 Timothy 4:13; Hebrews 10:25.

14. The gift of faith: Acts 11:22–24; Romans 4:18–21; 1 Corinthians 12:9; Hebrews 11.

15. The gift of hospitality: Acts 16:14–15; Romans 12:9–13; 16:23; Hebrews 13:1–2; 1 Peter 4:9.

16. The gift of mercy: Matthew 25:34–36; Luke 10:30–37; Romans 12:8.

17. The gift of giving: Mark 12:41–44; Romans 12:8; 2 Corinthians 8:1–7; 9:2–8.

18. The gift of prayer: Colossians 1:9–12; 4:12–13; 1 Timothy 2:1–2; James 5:14–16.

19. The gift of helping: Acts 9:36; Romans 16:1–2; 1 Corinthians 12:28.

20. The gift of teaching: Acts 18:24–28; 20:20–21; Romans 12:7; 1 Corinthians 12:28; Ephesians 4:11–14.

21. The gift of evangelism: Luke 19:1–10; 2 Timothy 4:5.

22. It is at Waypoint 7, "New Birth," that a traveler receives these gifts:
   - Gifts, as listed in this chapter, are from God (Rom. 12:5–6; 1 Cor. 12:18; 1 Pet. 4:10).
   - These gifts were given so that travelers can serve others (Rom. 12:6; 1 Cor. 12:7, 18).
   - The giving of these gifts occurs after new birth (1 Pet. 4:10).

23. Isaiah 41:10 MSG.

24. Psalm 34:17 MSG.

25. Luke 12:29–31.

26. Philippians 4:13.

27. 1 Corinthians 6:9–11 MSG.

CHAPTER 4

1. The apostle Paul in Romans 5:8 MSG.

2. This is a fictional encounter about a real event. Rev. Dr. Stuart Hoke was the Staff Chaplain of Trinity Episcopal Church on Wall Street at the time of the collapse of the World Trade Center in New York City. Though Dr. Hoke did not encounter Oksana (a fictional character), he did survive many of the events described in this chapter's story. Dr. Hoke often tells his remarkable and engaging story of how God worked through many ordinary people caught in the midst of unfathomable calamity.

3. Psalm 94:18–19, 22.

4. 2 Samuel 22:17–19.

5. Romans 4:17–18, 20–21 MSG.

6. In addition to the many Bible passages that refer to God as a heavenly Father, sometimes the Bible refers to God as having the traits of a loving mother (Isa. 42:14–15; 49:15; 66:13; Matt. 23:37; James 1:18). At other times the Bible refers to God as both heavenly father and mother (Deut. 32:10–11, 18; Ps. 27:10). The purpose of such passages is to remind the traveler that God offers to his children the best traits of both fatherhood and motherhood. For more on how God is described in the Bible as a loving parent, see Bob Whitesel, "The Pattern of Parenting" in *Preparing for Change Reaction: How to Introduce Change to Your Church* (Indianapolis, Ind.: Wesleyan Publishing House, 2008), 119–126.

7. 1 John 3:1 MSG.

8. Galatians 4:6–7 MSG.

9. Hebrews 4:15.

10. In theological terms, this means every person on the journey is a sinner. As James Engel states, "a person who is captive to self navigating . . . can never please God." James Engel, *Contemporary Christian Communication* (Nashville: Thomas Nelson, 1979), 211.

11. Isaiah 59:2 MSG.

12. 1 John 1:8–9 MSG.

13. Romans 3:23.

14. John 3:16 MSG.

15. Romans 3:23–24 MSG.

16. Romans 5:8.

17. Romans 6:23 MSG.

18. Hebrews 2:9–11.

19. John 14:6.

20. John 14:6–7 MSG.

21. Joshua 24:15.

22. Revelation 3:20.

23. Romans 10:13.

24. John 1:12.

25. Matthew 8:22 MSG.

CHAPTER 5

1. Romans 5:8 MSG.

2. Indian Point Presbyterian Church, www.indianpointchurch.org.

3. *Metanoia* is the Greek word used in the Scriptures for repentance, which "conveys the idea of turning, but focuses on the inner, cognitive decision to make a break with the past," according to Richard Peace, "Conflicting Understandings of Christian Conversion," vol. 2, no. 1 (New Haven, Conn.: International Bulletin of Missionary Research), 8.

4. *Pistis* is the Greek for "faith, trust, confidence in God" and conveys a reliance and assurance in God that can lead to conversion. Walter Bauer, *A*

Greek-English Lexicon of the New Testament and Other Early Christian Literature, eds. William F. Ardnt and F. Wilbur Gingrich (Chicago: University of Chicago Press, 1952), 668–670.

5. *Epistrophe* is the Greek term for conversion, and means to "turn around . . . a change of mind . . . [to turn] from something to something [else]." Bauer, *A Greek-English Lexicon of the New Testament*, 301. Peace notes this is a "reversing direction and going the opposite way," in "Conflicting Understandings of Christian Conversion," 8.

6. The first portion of this quote, attributed to the fictional Father Henry, is actually a quote by Paulist Fathers Kenneth Boyack, C.S.P. and Frank DeSiano, C.S.P., *Creating the Evangelizing Parish* (Mahwah, N. J.: Paulist Press, 1993), 39.

7. An excellent book that examines biblically and historically the rationale and requirements of God's holiness is Keith Drury, *Holiness for Ordinary People* 25th Anniversary ed. (Indianapolis, Ind.: Wesleyan Publishing House, 2009). See especially the chapter 2, "It's Everywhere," for a biblical examination of the scope of holiness.

8. 1 Peter 1:15–16 MSG.

9. 1 Timothy 4:8.

10. James 4:7–10.

11. Matthew 7:21–23 MSG.

12. Therefore, the supernatural should be allowed, even expected, to participate and guide the process. This does not mean sanctioning spiritual anarchy. Paul, in writing to the Corinthians, a church struggling with spiritual disorder and chaos, emphasized that God works in a logical and reasonable manner, stating, "But everything should be done in a fitting and orderly way" (1 Cor. 14:40).

13. Ephesians 2:8–10.

14. Ephesians 2:8–10 MSG.

15. Though there are different theological options regarding the degree to which choice is involved in human decisions, free will does exist at the point of decision. See James Engel, *Contemporary Christian Communication* (Nashville: Thomas Nelson, 1979), 211.

16. Here, Paul emphasized that faith and repentance result in a conversion, "a turn around . . . a change of mind . . . [to turn] from something to something [else)]. See Bauer, *A Greek-English Lexicon of the New Testament*, 301. In addition, Paul emphasizes that such a turnaround should be conspicuous. Various forms of declaration are often exhibited at this juncture. And, declaratory actions that accompany conversion are as diverse as cultures. In modernist societies shaped by education, a testimony might be expected; whereas, in postmodern environs influenced by action, serving others might be anticipated. For more on the behavioral differences between modernist/postmodernist cultures and their impact upon explaining the good news, see Bob Whitesel, *Preparing for Change Reaction: How to Introduce Change to Your*

Church (Indianapolis, Ind.: Wesleyan Publishing House, 2008), 49–71; *Inside the Organic Church: Learning from 12 Emerging Congregations* (Nashville: Abingdon Press, 2006), xxiii–xxxiii, and Bob Whitesel and Kent R. Hunter, *A House Divided: Bridging the Generation Gaps in Your Church* (Nashville: Abingdon Press, 2000), 13–81.

17. Engel, *Contemporary Christian Communication*, 211.

18. Ibid.

19. What kind of conversion are we talking about? I will limit this present discussion to conversion to Christianity. There is an abundance of literature dealing with different types of conversion, and I'm indebted to Richard Peace for classifying these varieties (Richard Peace, *Conversion in the New Testament: Paul and the Twelve* [Grand Rapids, Mich.: Eerdmans, 1999], 7–11). There are secular conversions, where a drug addict might be transformed from drug dependence to a drug-free lifestyle. There are manipulative conversions, where coercion is used by a cult or a government. There is conversion between religious worldviews, for instance the conversion from Sikhism to Hinduism that is taking place in India. And there is conversion from one Christian denomination to another, for instance when popular Catholic priest Rev. Alberto Cutie (nicknamed "Father Oprah") converted to the U.S. Episcopal denomination. Though all of these areas are of interest to scholars and researchers, we will limit this discussion to conversion to Christianity.

20. John 3:7–8 MSG.

21. "Our History," Plymouth Church of the Pilgrims, http://plymouth church.org/our_history.php.

22. 2 Corinthians 5:17 MSG.

23. A look at church history reveals that there are a wide range of experiences, tempos, and progressions associated with conversion. For examples of the range and variety in Christian conversionary experiences, see Hugh T. Kerr and John M. Mulder, eds., *Conversions: The Christian Experience* (Grand Rapids, Mich.: Eerdmans, 1983). However, there are common characteristics and elements that run through all of these conversations. Philosopher William James best summed up these common aspects when he described conversion as follows:

> To be converted, to be regenerated, to receive grace, to experience religion, to gain an assurance, are so many phrases which denote the process, gradual or sudden, by which a self hitherto divided, and consciously wrong, interior and unhappy, becomes unified and consciously right, superior and happy, in consequence of its firmer hold upon religious realities." (Quoted by Jacob W. Heikkinen, "Conversion: A Biblical Study," *National Faith and Order Colloquium*, World Council of Churches [June 12–17, 1966], 1.)

The Bible uses several Greek words to describe this conversion process. Each of these terms will help us more accurately understand conversion. Combining these three terms is important to understanding the matrix of conversion. Peace sums this up stating, "*Metanoia* (repentance) must be combined with *pistis* (faith) in order to bring about *epistophe* (conversion)." Peace, "Conflicting Understandings of Christian Conversion," 8.

24. Bauer, *A Greek-English Lexicon of the New Testament*, 301.

25. How and when does conversion occur? Does conversion occur in a flash, with miraculous transformations and heavenly encounters? Does conversion take place over time? Or perhaps conversion is a stumbling process, where the conversionary experience takes place in what Richard Peace calls "fits and starts." Richard Peace, Scot McKnight, and others have looked at the New Testament record and conclude that the answer is "all of the above." For further information on the topic of conversion, see the following publications: Charles Kraft, "Christian Conversion as a Dynamic Process," *International Christian Broadcasters Bulletin* (Colorado Springs: International Christian Broadcasters, 1974), Second Quarter; Scot McKnight, *Turning to Jesus: The Sociology of Conversion in the Gospels* (Louisville: Westminster John Knox Press, 2002); Richard Peace, *Conversion in the New Testament*, 6; Peace, "Conflicting Understandings of Christian Conversion"; Lewis R. Rambo, *Understanding Religious Conversion* (New Haven, Conn.: Yale University Press, 1993).

26. For a comparison of conversion experiences, see Figure 7.1 in my book *Spiritual Waypoints: Helping Others Navigate the Journey* (Indianapolis, Ind.: Wesleyan Publishing House, 2010), 142.

	Types of Conversion		
	Sudden Conversion	**Socialization**	**Liturgical Acts**
Oksana's friends	Martin	Reverend Stuart	Father Henry
Customary Denominational Context	Evangelicals,[ce] Pentecostals[ce]	Mainline Protestants[ce]	Roman Catholics,[ce] Orthodox Church[ce]
Strengths	Radical departure from the past.	Point of conversion does not require a sordid past.	Mystery and encounter with the supernatural.
Weaknesses	In some studies, only 10 percent of these decisions "resulted in long-term changes in personal behavior.[d] Mechanical tools can replace community.[e]	The work of conversion can "drift from the center of one's ecclesiastical vision."[e] Faith can become a matter of duty and obligation.[e]	Liturgy has to be learned, as well as how to participate in it before conversion.[e]

	Types of Conversion		
	Sudden Conversion	**Socialization**	**Liturgical Acts**
Adage	"Conversion is an individual experience that can be dated exactly."[e]	"Belonging before believing."[e]	"To arouse the sleeping faith in the nominal Christian."[e]
Customary participants	Raised in a secular environment.[e] First-generation Christians.[a]	Raised in a Christian home.[b] Second-generation Christians.[a]	Second-generation Christians.[a]

a. Charles Kraft, "Christian Conversion as a Dynamic Process," in *International Christian Broadcasters Bulletin* (Colorado Springs: International Christian Broadcasters, 1974), Second Quarter.
b. Scot McKnight, Personal Interview, June 2, 2009.
c. Scot McKnight, *Turning to Jesus: The Sociology of Conversion in the Gospels* (Louisville, Ky.: Westminster John Knox Press, 2002).
d. Donald Miller, *Reinventing American Protestantism: Christianity in the New Millennium* (Berkley: University of California Press, 1997), 171–172.
e. Richard Peace, "Conflicting Understandings of Christian Conversion: A Missiological Challenge," in *International Bulletin of Missionary Research*, vol. 28, No. 1, 8.

27. Colossians 3:17 MSG.

CHAPTER 6

1. Leo F. Buscaglia, *Love: What Life Is All About* (New York: Ballantine Books, 1996), 55.
2. Mark 10:29–30 MSG.
3. Psalm 41:9–10 MSG.
4. Hebrews 11:32–33, 36–38 MSG.
5. Romans 12:14.
6. Romans 12:17.
7. Billy Graham, *Just As I Am: The Autobiography of Billy Graham* (New York: HarperOne, 2007), 31.
8. 2 Corinthians 4:16–18 MSG.
9. Jeremiah 29:11.
10. 2 Corinthians 5:4–5 MSG.
11. Psalm 46:1.
12. Psalm 37:23–24 MSG.
13. Proverbs 1:33 MSG.
14. John 16:33.
15. Matthew 18:19–20 MSG.

16. The apostle Paul's most common description for a church is "Christ's body." See George Elton Ladd, *A Theology of the New Testament* (Grand Rapids, Mich.: Eerdmans, 1974), 545.

17. For more on the organic nature of the church, see Bob Whitesel, *Inside the Organic Church: Learning from 12 Emerging Congregations* (Nashville: Abingdon Press, 2006), xxiv–xxxviii.

18. 1 Corinthians 12:25–26 MSG.

19. Titus 2; St. Thomas' Church of Sheffield England created an innovative solution to create "extended families" for attendees who did not have biological families nearby. Once a month, the church combines or "clusters" three to five small groups (Bob Whitesel, "The Perfect Cluster: For Young Adults, St. Tom's, Sheffield Creates Extended Families, And Everyone Knows Where They Fit" in *Outreach Magazine* [Vista, Calif.: Outreach Inc.], 2005, vol. 4, Issue 3, 112–114). According to former Rector Mike Breen, these clusters "create an extended family feel, like the movie, *My Big Fat Greek Wedding*" (Mike Breen, personal conversation with the author, Sheffield, England, May 20, 2004). It is in these clusters (numbering between thirty-five and seventy-five people) that congregants at St. Thomas' have come together once a month to socialize, serve the needy, and grow in Christ.

20. I have suggested that the healthiest model for most churches will be a multi-generational structure. Kent Hunter and I have described seven steps for growing a multi-generational church in Whitesel and Hunter, *A House Divided: Bridging the Generation Gaps in Your Church* (Nashville: Abingdon Press, 2000).

21. Romans 12:4–5 MSG.

22. 1 Corinthians 12:7 MSG.

23. 1 Corinthians 12:27 MSG.

24. Hebrews 10:25.

25. James 1:27 MSG.

26. Mark 9:35.

27. Matthew 5:16.

28. Matthew 5:16 MSG.

CHAPTER 7

1. Mohandas Karamchand Gandhi, as quoted by William Rees-Mogg in *The Times* [London] (4 April 2005), 12. Gandhi is referring to the statement of Jesus in Luke 16:13 that, "No servant can serve two masters. Either he will hate the one and love the other, or he will be devoted to the one and despise the other. You cannot serve both God and Money."

2. Though other scriptural passages provide fitting examples of the spiritual foundations of the traveler, to keep the scriptural references from becoming too vast, I will limit my references to the gospel of Mark. This was done

for two reasons. First, Mark provides the most concise description of Jesus' ministry and is a suitable and comprehensive overview for a new disciple. Second, Mark underscores the progressive nature of the disciples' belief. For a thorough examination of Mark in relationship to the conversion of the disciples see, Richard Peace, *Conversion in the New Testament: Paul and the Twelve* (Grand Rapids, Mich.: Eerdmans, 1999), 105–281, 319–329.

3. Selected examples in the gospel of Mark include: 2:13–28; 9:33–37, 41; 10:35–45; 12:28–34.

4. Selected examples in the gospel of Mark include: 3:1–6; 4:35–41; 5:1–43; 6:30–52; 9:14–29; 10:46–52.

5. Selected examples in the gospel of Mark include: 1:1–11; 8:27–30, 36–38; 9:1–12; 12:35–37; 13:24–37; 14:62.

6. Selected examples in the gospel of Mark include: 2:9–10, 17; 3:23–29; 10:13–16, 31; 11:25; 14:22–26; 16:1–20.

7. Selected examples in the gospel of Mark include: 1:16–20; 2:13–17; 3:13–19; 6:6–13; 8:34–38; 14:27–31; 16:15–20.

8. Selected examples in the gospel of Mark include: 2:17; 7:1–23; 8:34–38; 9:42–50; 10:1–12, 17–31; 11:15–19; 14:37–38.

9. Jim Dunn, "The Process of Spiritual Formation," letter to the author, nd.

10. 2 Corinthians 5:17.

11. Jesus exemplified serving others. Selected examples in the gospel of Mark include: 2:13–28; 9:33–37, 41; 10:35–45; 12:28–34.

12. Galatians 5:22–23.

13. This figure was developed by Dunn, "Process."

14. There is a misperception that small groups are a ministry program comprised of home fellowship groups that meet on weeknights for church members. While there are such programs, a small group should actually be thought of as "any small group of three to twelve people formally or informally meeting approximately one or more times a month within the church fellowship network," Bob Whitesel, *Growth By Accident, Death By Planning: How Not to Kill a Growing Congregation* (Nashville: Abingdon Press, 2004), 139–140. Small groups include: Sunday school classes; Bible studies; leadership committees; classes of any kind; prayer groups; praise teams; or any kind of church team (ministry, fellowship, or athletic orientated).

15. Even secular researchers such as Peter Block agree, "The small group is the unit of transformation." Peter Block, *Community: The Struggle of Belonging* (San Francisco: Berrett-Koehler, 2008), 95.

16. Matthew 10:1; 20:17; Mark 3:14; 6:7; Luke 6:13.

17. Mike Breen first proposed the triangle in *Outside In: Reaching Unchurched Young People Today* (Bletchley, United Kingdom: Scripture Union Publishing, 2003), and later developed the triangle and accompanying icons into a discipleship tool called "LifeShapes." For more information about

LifeShapes see Mike Breen and Walk Kallestad, *The Passionate Church: The Art of Lifechanging Discipleship* (Colorado Springs: Cook Publications, 2005). For an overview of the Lifeshape icons see Bob Whitesel, *Inside the Organic Church: Learning from 12 Emerging Congregations* (Nashville: Abingdon Press, 2006), 6–8.

18. Paddy Mallon wrote an engaging look at the growth of St. Thomas' Church to England's largest Anglican congregation with most of the attendees under thirty-five years of age in *Calling a City Back to God* (Eastbourne, United Kingdom: Kingsway Publishers, 2003).

19. Sometimes the OUT or outreach element of small groups is the most difficult to foster. Some small groups are effectively closed to outsiders, often because the small group has shared personal challenges and they resist the idea of sharing these too publically. Thus, a small group, even without realizing it, may not make newcomers feel welcome. This may be permissible for small groups with attendees struggling with personal and confidential life issues. Still, these groups should be engaged in some outreach in order to maintain a healthy balance in the triangle of UP-IN-OUT. If they do not maintain this balance, they can become self-centered rather than serving others. Mike Breen's congregation in Sheffield, England, overcame this problem by combining three to five small groups into an outreach and service cluster (Breen and Bob Hopkins, *Clusters: Creative Mid-Sized Missional Communities* [Sheffield, United Kingdom: Anglican Church Planting Initiatives, 2008]). These clusters range in size from thirty-five to seventy-five and provide a good-sized force for social service ministries. In addition, Breen found that clusters which met once a month were better venues for reaching out to newcomers and helping them find a suitable small group. When three to five small groups are clustered, the newcomer can participate in the cluster and through relationships discover which small group is best for them. Breen also said, "People don't feel they lost their friends when they start a new small group, and some members of their group leaves to help start it. They still see each other in the monthly cluster meetings, and they don't feel like they've lost their former small group friends" (Mike Breen, personal conversation, Sheffield, United Kingdom, June 10, 2009).

20. In addition to not having enough small groups, the other weakness that undermines healthy churches today is not having robust prayer ministries toward both the church and unchurched. To foster such balanced prayer ministry, see Whitesel, *Growth By Accident, Death By Planning*, "Missteps With Prayer," 43–54; and Bob Whitesel and Kent R. Hunter, *A House Divided: Bridging the Generation Gaps in Your Church*, "Step 7: Mobilizing Your Church for Transgenerational Prayer" (Nashville: Abingdon Press, 2000), 222–237. Also, see Elmer Towns's exhaustive study on the correlation between church growth and prayer in *Praying the Lord's Prayer for Spiritual Breakthrough* (Ventura, Calif.: Gospel Light Publications 1997); *How to Pray When You*

Don't Know What to Say: More Than 40 Ways to Approach God (Ventura, Calif.: Regal, 2006); and *Prayer Partners: How to Increase the Power and Joy of Your Prayer Life by Praying with Others* (Ventura, Calif.: Regal, 2006).
21. Nelle Connally and Mickey Herskowitz, *From Love Field: Our Final Hours with President John F. Kennedy* (New York: Rugged Land, 2003), 180.
22. Matthew 10:1–42; Mark 6:6–13; Luke 10:1–24.
23. 1 Samuel 2:3; 1 Chronicles 28:9; John 16:30.
24. Matthew 4:18–20; 8:20.
25. Mark 1:16–20.
26. Mark 1:29–45.
27. Matthew 17:16–19.
28. Mark 6:30; Luke 9:10.
29. Matthew 17:16–21.
30. Matthew 4:1–11.

CHAPTER 8

1. Rod Stewart and Ron Wood, "Every Picture Tells a Story," album by the same title (Los Angeles: Polygram Records, 1971).
2. Richard Houts originally published his thoughts about a "Spiritual Gift Inventory" in *Eternity Magazine* (Philadelphia: Evangelical Foundation, 1976). He also penned the *Houts Inventory of Spiritual Gifts: A Self-assessment Instrument to Help Ascertain Your Ministry Gift, or Gifts, and the Related Opportunities for Christian Service* (Pasadena, Calif.: Fuller Evangelistic Association, 1985). Other authors have adapted the Houts questionnaire to specific audiences and denominational perspectives, including Ruth Towns and Elmer Towns, *Women Gifted For Ministry: How To Discover and Practice Your Spiritual Gifts* (Nashville: Thomas Nelson, 2001); David Stark, Sandra Hirsch, and Jane Kise, *LifeKeys: Discovering Who You Are* (Minneapolis, Minn.: Bethany House Publishers, 2005); Aubrey Malphurs, *Maximizing Your Effectiveness* (Grand Rapids, Mich: Baker Books, 2006), 199–208; Larry Gilbert, *Spiritual Gifts Inventory: Discover Your Spiritual Gift in Only 20 Minutes* (Elkton, Md.: Church Growth Institute, 1999); and specifically for teens Jane Kise and Kevin Johnson, *Find Your Fit: Dare to Act on God's Gift for You* (Minneapolis, Minn.: Bethany House Publishers, 1999).
3. 1 Corinthians 12:4–8 MSG.
4. James 1:27 MSG.
5. Clinton states that at this waypoint, the leader now "recognizes that part of God's guidance for ministry comes through establishing ministry priorities by discerning gifts." J. Robert Clinton, *The Making of a Leader: Recognizing the Lessons and Stages of Leadership Development* (Colorado Springs: NavPress, 1988), 32.
6. Leadership writer Peter Northouse describes traits, abilities, skills, and behaviors as the basic building blocks of leadership (*Introduction to*

Leadership: Concepts and Precepts [Thousand Oaks, Calif.: SAGE Publications, 2009], 2–3). Traits are inherent and endowed qualities; abilities are aptitudes developed by experience; skills are methods for carrying out leadership; and behaviors are what leaders do with traits, abilities, and skills. Northouse makes a persuasive argument that all leaders develop these elements of leadership. First Corinthians 12:7; Ephesians 4:7; and 1 Peter 4:10 appear to indicate that such predilections take on supernatural vigor when empowered by the Holy Spirit.

7. Adapted from the United Methodist Church's *Explore Your Spiritual Gifts* (http://www.umc.org/site/c.lwL4KnN1LtH/b.1355371/k.9501/Spiritual_Gifts.htm, 2009); Jack W. MacGorman's *The Gifts of the Spirit* (Nashville: Broadman Press, 1974); Kenneth C. Kinghorn's *Gifts of the Spirit* (Nashville: Abingdon Press, 1976); and C. Peter Wagner's *Your Spiritual Gifts Can Help Your Church Grow: How to Find Your Gifts and Use Them to Bless Others* (Ventura, Calif.: Regal Books, 1994). Note that the list tendered here is not definitive or exhaustive. Rather, it is a codification of the above gift inventories and is designed to provide a holistic list for Christian communities seeking to help travelers at Waypoint 2. For a chart of the gifts correlated with their biblical attestations, see George Elton Ladd, *A Theology of the New Testament* (Grand Rapids, Mich.: Eerdmans, 1974), 534–535.

8. The gift of hospitality is often primarily associated, though erroneously, with church assimilation programs such as hosting newcomer tables, or greeting church visitors. However, when the Scriptures discuss the gift of hospitality, something more radical and basic is indicated by the context. For example, Peter admonishes the church in 1 Peter 1:9 to offer hospitality in scenarios where grumbling might be the normal reaction. The context of Peter's admonition (1 Pet. 1:1–11) indicates that Peter is talking about giving hospitality not only to the Christians, but also to those who heap abuse upon Christians. Such radical hospitality means meeting what Maslow described as physiological and safety needs before people are ready to have their needs met for belongingness and love met (Abraham H. Maslow, *Motivation and Personality* [New York: HarperCollins, 1987], 300–394; and Abraham H. Maslow, *The Farther Reaches of Human Nature* [New York: Penguin Press, 1993], 300).

9. This is a gift for which there are several interpretations. Assemblies of God writer Donald Gee sees the gift of knowledge as a supernatural forthtelling; Donald Gee, *Concerning Spiritual Gifts* (Springfield, Mo.: Gospel Publishing House, 1972). Others like Wagner (*Your Spiritual Gifts Can Help Your Church Grow*) take a less supernatural route, noting that "those who have this gift are superior learners" (190). It is not my intention to side with one interpretation over the other, for readers from various backgrounds and theology will use this book. Therefore, this book is designed to describe the gifts from varying perspectives, to allow the you to embrace the interpretation that best fits your understanding, tradition, and theology.

10. Here again there are several perspectives. For examples of the differences see Donald Gee's *Concerning Spiritual Gifts* and Kinghorn's *Gifts of the Spirit*.

11. The gift of service is sometimes attached too exclusively to administrative tasks (*Your Spiritual Gifts Can Help Your Church Grow*, 258), when in the context of verses such as 2 Timothy 1:16–18, the gift of service indicates organizing to meet the needs of all others. Thus, the gift of service should not be primarily a service to the church, but equally indicate serving the needs of those outside the church.

12. This is another gift which has a more supernatural tenor in Donald Gee's *Concerning Spiritual Gifts*. Kinghorn (*Gifts of the Spirit*) and Wagner (*Your Spiritual Gifts Can Help Your Church Grow*) see the gift of wisdom differently, as those possessing insight and perception into problems and solutions.

13. See the United Methodist Church's definition in "Explore Your Spiritual Gifts," http://www.umc.org/site/c.lwL4KnN1LtH/b.1355371/k.9501/Spiritual_Gifts.htm.

14. Regarding this gift, see Wagner's *Your Spiritual Gifts Can Help Your Church Grow* for a Charismatic viewpoint and Gee's *Concerning Spiritual Gifts* for a Classical Pentecostal viewpoint on this gift.

15. The Charismatic and Classical Pentecostal viewpoints are best described by Wagner in *Your Spiritual Gifts Can Help Your Church Grow*, 256–257.

16. For another viewpoint of this and other gifts see the United Methodist Church's definitions in "Explore Your Spiritual Gifts," http://www.umc.org/site/c.lwL4KnN1LtH/b.1355371/k.9501/Spiritual_Gifts.htm.

17. For the stories of five missionary martyrs, see Wagner, *Your Spiritual Gifts Can Help Your Church Grow*, 62–63.

18. Some authors list craftsmanship and music as gifts of the Holy Spirit (c.f. Christian A. Schwarz, *The 3 Colors of Ministry* [St. Charles, Ill.: ChurchSmart Resources, 2001], 157), but these designations are actually sub-categories of artist. To use these sub-categories ignores the important scriptural attestations to the Old Testament artisans who worked in varied crafts and mediums. Thus, for a more holistic understanding "artist" better sums up this categorical gift.

19. Ray C. Stedman, *Body Life* (Ventura, Calif.: Regal Books, 1972), 54.

20. Matthew 7:11.

21. Findley B. Edge, *The Greening of the Church* (Dallas, Tex.: Word, 1971), 141.

22. 1 Corinthians 12:7; 1 Peter 4:10.

CHAPTER 9

1. Rick Warren, interview by Ann Curry, "Rick Warren: Pastor in the Political Spotlight," *Dateline NBC*, Dec. 19, 2008.

2. For the latest secular research into elements of authenticity in leadership, see Bruce J. Avolio and William L. Gardner, "Authentic Leadership

Development: Getting to the Root of Positive Forms of Leadership" in *The Leadership Quarterly* 16, no. 3 (June 2005): 315–338.

3. For more on strategic, tactical, and operational leadership, including a questionnaire to see which traits you or your leaders exhibit, see Bob Whitesel, *Preparing for Change Reaction: How to Introduce Change in Your Church*, (Indianapolis, Ind.: Wesleyan Publishing House, 2007), 29–48.

4. Whitesel, *Preparing for Change Reaction*, 37.

5. Fred Luthans and Bruce Avolio, "Authentic Leadership: A Positive Development Approach" in Kim S. Cameron, Jane E. Dutton, and Robert E. Quinn, eds. *Positive Organizational Scholarship: Foundations of a New Discipline* (San Francisco, Calif.: Berrett-Koehler, 2003), 243.

6. Bob Whitesel, *Inside the Organic Church: Learning from 12 Emerging Congregations* (Nashville: Abingdon Press, 2006), 133–134.

7. Luthans and Avolio, *The High Impact Leader*, 94–95.

CHAPTER 10

1. George Bernard Shaw, commenting upon the outlook of John Bunyan's hero, Christian, as Christian looked back from the "brink of the river of death over the strife and labor of his pilgrimage," from "Man and Superman," in *Plays by George Bernard Shaw* (New York: Signet Classics, 1960), 257.

2. J. Robert Clinton, *The Making of a Leader: Recognizing the Lessons and Stages of Leadership Development* (Colorado Springs: NavPress, 1988), 33.

3. 2 Timothy 3:16 MSG.

AFTERWORD

1. James 1:26–27 MSG.

2. Matthew 22:37–40.

3. John 14:6.

4. George Bernard Shaw, from "Man and Superman," in *Plays by George Bernard Shaw* (New York: Signet Classics, 1960), 257.